Fel

CLASSICS OF RUSSIAN POETRY

Boris Pasternak

POEMS

BORIS PASTERNAK

Poems

*translated from the Russian
by Eugene M. Kayden*

Second Edition
Revised and Enlarged

The Antioch Press
Yellow Springs, Ohio • 1964

All royalty payments accruing to the translator from the publication of the first edition of *Poems* by Boris Pasternak have been pledged by him to the second edition and to the publication of translations from Pushkin and Lermontov as his contribution to fruitful cultural relations between the people of the United States and the Soviet Union.

First edition, *Poems,* published by The University of Michigan Press, October, 1959. Second edition, *Poems,* revised and enlarged, published by the Antioch Press, February, 1964. Copyright 1964 by Eugene M. Kayden. Library of Congress Catalog Card No. 63-14379. Manufactured in the United States of America by The Antioch Press, Yellow Springs, Ohio.

I Dedicate these Translations
to my Father and Mother
In Memoriam

Contents

ACKNOWLEDGMENTS xv
FOREWORD xvii

MY SISTER LIFE

In Memory of *The Demon* 3
About My Verses 4
My Sister Life 5
The Weeping Garden 6
Dawnlight 7
Out of Superstition 8
"Fresh Paint" 9
Patterns 10
Swaying On a Bough 12
Resting Oars 13
Spring Rainstorm 14
Stars in Summertime 15
An English Lesson 16
Definition of Poetry 17
Definition of the Soul 18
Definition of Creative Art 19
Our Thunderstorm 20
Sparrow Hills 22
Disagreement 23
Sultry Night 25
A Still More Sultry Dawn 26
Moochkap 28
Home at Last 29
Summer 1917 30
Summer Thunderstorm 31

Darling, It Frightens Me! 32
Let's Strew Our Words 33
Postscript 35

THEMES AND VARIATIONS

Encounter 39
Mephistopheles 41
Shakespeare 42
A Theme With Variations:
    The Theme 44
    1. Original Variation 46
    2. Derivative Variation 47
    3. The Racing Stars 50
    4. Clouds. And Stars. 51
    5. Gypsy Splendor 52
    6. The Sunset Steppe 53
That May Happen 54
January 1919 56
Lovers' Quarrel:
    1. O Treacherous Angel 57
    2. O the Shame! 57
    3. I'll Free Myself 58
    4. Stop Me If You Dare! 58
    5. Entwine This Shower 59
    6. Disillusioned? 59
    7. My Darling, Dearest! 60
    8. My Table's Not Wide Enough 60
    9. The Trembling Piano 61
You Think I Could Forget? 62
Thus Life Begins 63
We Are Few 64

My Pictures Swing 65
In The Wood 66
The House at Spásskoye 67
So Be It 68
It's Spring Out There 69
Drizzling Rains 70
Poetry 71
Enigma's Fingernail Mark 72

POEMS OF TWO REVOLUTIONS

A Woman Revolutionary 75
Bloody Sunday 76
Mutiny at Sea 80
A Testament 87
Sublime Malady 89

ABOVE THE BARRIERS

The Drowsy Garden 103
Winter Skies 104
The Soul 105
Snow Storm 106
The Urals for the First Time 107
Spring Days 108
Three Movements 109
Improvistation 111
To a Friend 112
To Anna Akhmátova 113
To M. T. 115
Balzac 117
Sailing Away 119
O Great Marksman 121

Cocks 122
Lilies of the Valley 123
Lyubka 124

SECOND BIRTH

Waves:
1. Here All Things Meet 127
2. I Would Go Home Again 128
3. We Came to Georgia 130
4. The Caucasus 131
5. Socialism 132
6. Things of Great Worth 133
The Death of a Poet 135
Don't Worry About Me 136
Dear Love's a Heavy Cross 137
And Still It Snows! 138
Darkness of Death 139
Gay Shawls and Shoes 141
The Fumes of Vain Renown 142
O Love, My Best 143
There's No One in That House 145
You're Here at Last 146
Vision of Tiflis 147
Had I Known It Once for All 149
When I Grow Weary 150
Hurry, My Verses, Hurry! 151

EARLY TRAINS and THE VAST EARTH

The Poet's Stubborn Temper 155
Ages. He Appears. 156
How Good to Be of a Piece 158

Summer Day 159
The Pines 160
False Alarm 162
Early Winter Days 164
Hoarfrost 165
A Sentimental Waltz 167
On Early Trains 169
Thrushes 171
The Tragic Story 173
The Conqueror 174
Spring 1944 175

THE POEMS OF DOCTOR ZHIVAGO

Hamlet 179
March 180
Holy Week 181
White Night 184
Spring Floods 186
Explanation 188
Summer in the City 190
Winds 191
Intoxication 192
False Summer 193
The Wedding Party 194
Autumn 197
A Fairy Tale 199
August 203
Winter Night 205
Parting 207
Meeting 209
Star of the Nativity 211

Dawn 215
The Miracle 217
Earth 219
Evil Days 221
Mary Magdalene I 223
Mary Magdalene II 225
Garden of Gethsemane 227

WHEN THE SKIES CLEAR

In All My Ways 233
Fame 235
The Soul 236
Eve 237
Without a Title 239
The Change 240
Spring in the Forest 241
July 242
After Mushrooms 244
Stillness 246
Hayricks 247
The Linden Avenue 248
Clear Skies Again 250
Bread 252
Autumn Woods 253
First Frosts 254
Night Wind 255
Golden Autumn 256
Foul Weather 258
Grass and Stones 259
Night 261

Wind (Four Fragments About Blok)
    1. Who Should Live 263
    2. He Is Like the Wind 264
    3. The Great Field 265
    4. The Horizon's On Fire 266
The Highway 267
In the Hospital 268
Music 270
After the Interval 272
First Snow 273
Snows Are Falling 274
Footprints in the Snow 276
After the Blizzard 277
Bacchanalia 278
Around the Turning 287
Fulfilment 289
Ploughing Time 291
The Journey 292
Women In My Childhood 294
The Passing Thunderstorm 296
Winter Holidays 297
Unique Days 299
The Nobel Prize 300
God's Great World 301

NOTES AND COMMENTS 303

ACKNOWLEDGMENTS

Every effort is here made to acknowledge the sources of the poetry embodied in this book of translations. The first basic source was Pasternak's *Stikhotvoréniya v odnóm tóme* (Poetry in One Volume) published by the Association of Leningrad Writers in 1933, a volume of 430 pages. For the wartime poetry, the translator is indebted to two small books, namely, *Na ránnikh poezdákh* (Early Trains, 1943) and *Zemnói prostór* (The Vast Earth, 1945).

Of the series *Stikhotvoréniya Yuriya Zhivágo* (The Poems of Doctor Zhivago) ten appeared in *Znamya* (April, 1954) prior to the publication of the novel, and two in *Den poézii* (Poetry Day, 1956). Individual poems of that series appeared at various times in *Nóvoye russkoye slovo*, *Russkaya mysl*, *Possév*, and other Russian emigre papers. The periodical *Grani* published fifteen poems in 1957 (issues 34, 35, 36). All of the Zhivago poems were circulating in Europe, separately from the novel, in the summer of 1957. The translator is grateful to PANTHEON PRESS, New York, for giving him a photostat copy of Pasternak's own typewritten manuscript, for comparison and verification with other sources, and also grateful to THE UNIVERSITY OF MICHIGAN PRESS for letting him have the Russian text embodied in the novel they had published (Ann Arbor, 1958).

Some of the poems of the last series, written in 1956-1959, collected under the general title *Kogdá razgulyáetsia* (When the Skies Clear) found their first publication in Russia: eight poems in *Znamya* (September 1956), one in *Novy mir* (October 1956) and two in *Den poezii* of 1957. The translator is especially indebted to Mr. Victor S. Frank for his generous gift of a photostat set of these 44 poems with corrections approved by Pasternak.

A new edition of selected poetry, with revisions, was in preparation in 1957 under Pasternak's supervision. It appeared in Moscow in 1961, entitled *Stikhotvoréniya i poémy* (Poems and Tales). The book of 375 pages included 35 of the poems of 1956-1959.

The translator's new edition, revised and enlarged (Antioch Press, 1963), has profited by Pasternak's new revisions, especially in the long poem, "Sublime Malady." He is also indebted to the Russian edition by Gleb Struve and Boris Filipoff (University of Michigan Press, 1961) for a number of lines as revised by Pasternak in 1957.

Above all, the translator feels grateful to Boris Pasternak himself who gave his permission and blessing to "proceed boldly" with the task of publication.

A number of translations in this volume have originally appeared in the following periodicals: *The New Statesman and Nation*, *The New Republic*, *The Colorado Quarterly*, *The Russian Review*, *Approach*, *The Christian Century*, and *The Sewanee Review*. Thanks are due to the publishers for their permission to reprint.

The manuscript poem, THE PASSING THUNDERSTORM, facing page 296, was a personal gift from Boris Pasternak to the translator in appreciation of his work. "Your translations of Summer 1917, Poetry, and 'Improvistation' moved me and I overcame my inveterate resistance against myself. Owing to you I felt for a moment anew the freshness and thrill of that past. I am happy to say it to you quite sincerely." (Letter, 20 April 1959). The original has been presented for permanent safekeeping to Harvard University, Library of Rare Books and Manuscripts.

As for the binding, Mr. Pasternak wrote to the translator: "My favorite combination of colors is dark violet and light yellow," in case there should be a new edition (Letter, 3 December, 1959). The Antioch Press is pleased to comply with his personal request.

Foreword

I had a brief exchange of letters with Boris Leonìdovich Pasternàk in the summer of 1958, before I had the privilege of reading his *Doctor Zhivago*. From his home in Peredélkino he wrote to me under date of 22 August 1958, a long letter evoked—and, in part, provoked—by a statement of mine that his real home remains poetry where his vision is personal and unique in its intensity. Yet I believe with Mr. Pasternak that the future has taken residence in the streets and byways of the world, that we are part of it, and I am filled with the "silent music of happiness" heard at the heart of his novel and poetry because of my humble submission to the mystery of life and my serene confidence in the dawn of the new dispensation of kindliness and love among men everywhere. I reproduce his letter, written in English, with a few minor excisions unrelated to the issue of his poetry.

"In your last and previous letters, in your short essay on Pushkin, in your translations of his poetry and in your work on my behalf, I do not find anything other than worthy aims and achievements. You say I am 'first and last a poet, a lyric poet.' Is it really so? And should I feel proud of being just that? And do you realize the meaning of my being no more than that, whereas it hurts me to feel that I have not had the ability to express in greater fullness the whole of poetry and life in their complete unity? But what am I without the novel, and what have you to write about me without drawing upon that work, its terms and revelations?

"I cannot say, like Mayakóvsky, let's have 'as many poets as possible, good and various others.' Against mere numbers, I should wish—not literally of course—that poets were few; the matter of their scarcity does not interest me much—but that one poet should be true and great, expressing supremely and inimitably the life of his age. Art is not simply a description of life, but a setting forth of the uniqueness of being. What we call the splendor and vividness of description is not a feature imputed merely to style, but something far greater, namely, the presence of a new conception and the philosophic sense of life's own oneness and wholeness. The significant writer of his epoch (and I want no other beside him) is a revelation, a representation of the unknown, unrepeatable uniqueness of living reality. What else is originality if not a cultural event having its source in the world's absolute total reality?

"Many forgotten periods of history were once thought to be the end of the world, like our present nuclear situation. Each age, each stage of historical existence is compounded of two terms, the known and the unrevealed. The latter is infinite and unknown, because the future is at all times a part of this unexplored and unknown infinity that I can speak of without resort to mysticism— the burgeoning, profound, momentous tomorrow.

"Each art, especially that of poetry, means a great deal more than it comprises. Its essence and values are symbolic. This does in no manner signify that we possess the key by which we can discover behind every word or condition some other hidden sense—mystical, occult, or providential—as was erroneously believed of the dramatic works of Ibsen, Maeterlinck, or Leonid Andréyev. Nor does it mean that each true, creative poetical text ought to be a parable or an allegory. What I want to say is that besides and above the separate tropes and metaphorical turns of a poem there exists a figurative tendency, a drift in the poetry itself and in art as a whole—and that is its chief significance—to relate the general, summary purport of a composition to broader and more fundamental ideas—in order to reveal the sublimity of life and the unfathomable values of human existence. I am tempted to say that art does not equal itself, does not mean itself alone, but that it means tangibly something beyond itself. In this way we call art symbolic in essence.

"If I believe an author is not too great in his natural endowments, or if I do not discover in his works this immense spiritual quality, this sense of all-surpassing, overarching importance to life, he is as nothing to me however good the written page. It is as if somebody began to scurry to and fro in an open field, waving flags and lights along the railway track, without a railway train in sight. Art is for me a manifestation and a symptom; it must show that we stand in the presence of new all-encompassing values, in the presence of the great.

"Beginning with Pushkin we have our Russian contemporaneity, the real and the true, our modern thinking and spiritual consciousness. Pushkin erected the house of our spiritual life, the edifice of Russia's historical awareness. Lermontov was its first tenant. In Lermontov we have the independent confessional note in the subsequent intellectual tradition of our century, in poetry and prose, later enriched by the magnificent concreteness of Leo Tolstoy, then Chekhov's sharp-eyed absolute sensitiveness to reality. But whereas Pushkin is objective, tangible, and just, with generalizations of the widest meaning, Lermontov is passionate and personal, and therefore more limited; whereas Pushkin is realistic and exalted in creative activity, Lermontov is its living personal testimony. And as you have stated it, his operatic romanticism is apparent in part. The influence of Byron was unmistakable, because half of Europe had been under his spell. But what we wrongly take for romanticism in Lermontov seems to me to be in fact the unbalanced nature of this modern personal biographical realism and the foreshadowing of our modern poetry and prose. I dedicated *My Sister Life* not to the memory of Lermontov but to the poet himself as though he were living in our midst—to his spirit still effectual in our literature. What was he to me, you ask, in the summer of 1917?—The personification of creative adventure and discovery, the principle of everyday free poetical statement."

I here allow myself a few comments on Pasternak's vision of poetry, with special regard to Pushkin and Lermontov. I have in mind his scope and freshness, his spacious seriousness, his personal heroism, and the poetic directness and serenity of his maturer work. As with other great Russian masters of prose and verse, to be an artist is to be intensely religious. Like Tolstoy's his work is infused with the sense of the totality of life, with social compassion and an anti-heroic philosophy of history. In him life draws the deeper breath. His physical objects are unvaryingly dynamic, with the immediacy of the material, and with their spiritual quintessence wonderfully in place, for so much is at stake beyond perceptive technical performance or inviolate lyric grace.

The poet's message, I understand Boris Leonidovich to say, is a special way of apprehension, an act of vision, which, like wisdom, is an act of love and compassion in human destiny. It is not, strictly speaking, an act of moral conversion, social aspiration, and justice, or political exhortation. The poet is unique because he speaks to us as free men with a sense of a revelation, that our sublime vision of life as an end in itself may not perish. His words demand our turning to the future that we may share a life of objective reality and truth. For this reason I have long regarded Mr. Pasternak as the greatest poet to emerge from the Revolution of 1917, as a man with roots deep down in Russia's cultural history, as a poet who has his "fame and partnership in homebred Russian art." I have shunned, in my translations of him, the literal and the neutral. I have preserved what is literary and ripe in contemporary speech. I have not aimed to make my versions faithful to schoolroom notions of cramped accuracy, but faithful to Pasternak's thought and sense of life. If I have at times narrowed the compass and delicacy of his lines, failed him in versatility, passion, and lyric loveliness, if I have not reached full accuracy, let alone perfection, I have at least lived with his mind and spirit for many years, made his growth my growth, fascinated by the imaginative color of the original and heartened in my timidity by his counsel—the hint of a translator to a fellow translator—to have the courage of imperfection.

Pasternak came in an age of religious and philosophic waywardness, at a time of estrangement between philosophy, science, social statesmanship, and the fine arts, at a time of great crisis, war, revolution, and social division embracing the whole of human life. It was a time when authority was feared or mistrusted, and every claim to absolute understanding under suspicion—the poet's claim in particular, a claim which proves itself only as deeper insight and perception, as a form of love, and as a commitment to freedom in the name of individual worth. This was Russia's heritage, glorified by Pushkin in his sonnet, *To the Poet,* in the name of the vision of life that must be worshipped:

> O Poet, believe not in the crowd's acclaim.
> Soon pass the noontide ecstasies of praise;
> The mob will mock you, fools their judgment raise.
> But live, unmoved, above their storm and blame,
> A king apart. Shine, Poet, in your fame!
> Go, free, in fearlessness, on splendid ways,
> Attaining mastery of thought and phrase,
> And for your noble work no payment claim.
> Your art alone your wage. O highest judge,
> And stern tribunal of your work entire,
> Are you content? Exacting craftsman, say,
> Is art enough? Then let the rabble grudge,
> And curse, and spit upon your altar fire,
> And shake your tripod in their childish play.

The poet's word is a revelation of the Eternal. This is Pasternak's meaning when he speaks of the art of Pushkin as "objective, tangible, and just" and as a poetic act "exalted in creative activity." Indeed, the poet is of this world and of the obdurate earth, a neighbor among neighbors, the closest of man's neighbors even in his aloofness. But the function of the poet is greater by far than the ways of nature, welfare, knowledge, and social progress. His intimations are not ordinary. His perceptions are unique and integral. But if he possesses no steady vision of reality he runs the hazard of brutish passivity, ambiguous impressionism, pointless rebellion, or destructive cynicism. He is then a disinherited spirit, the least in the world of men, as Pushkin has truly said, a man who has diminished himself.

No! The Poet's way is the way of insight, love, and revelation as the art of profoundest seeing, the way of the Eternal. He will "render to Caesar the things that are Caesar's, and to God the things that are God's." In a time of spiritual disorder it is his special task to cherish the individual soul as the supreme gift of being, to bear witness to his vision of life in all its diversities and wholeness. He cannot be commanded in the name of social welfare and progress. His choice must remain a personal choice, made in conscience and in freedom, out of his love for the whole of God's creation.

As a poet, Pasternak prefers Pushkin and Chekhov for their "blazing directness" and devotion to fact. He accepts life and exults in its manifestations. He does justice to the Revolution, "the wonderful, unforgettable era of new, permanent achievements," but he turns away from glittering ideological phrases mouthed by special pleaders. He bears witness to the history of our time, and his work is distinguished by two concepts without which modern man is unthinkable, namely, the idea of the free personality and of life regarded as a Christian service and sacrifice. Doctor Zhivago practiced that higher freedom, the gift of Christ to humanity, as he moved through sacrifice to victory over death,—the essence of Eternity.

"I cannot cross the road and go beyond the fence without treading upon the face of the universe," thus Pasternak speaks (*The Steppe*). He knows how intimate the union between things earthly and the Infinite. He knows, too, something of the sinister powers that rule society in the modern world. But he has serene faith in the life of man in civilization; he has sublimity in compassion and tenderness with growing things. Before the bar of earthly powers in technology and politics he is a poet who pleads for the future and for the unique qualities of personal and community life. He has seen the Burning Bush, and his appeal is to humanity everywhere —one and undivided. This adjuration cannot be confined to the Soviet Union alone. Pasternak's universal plea is for continuity, for a living relationship with the future, with nature and art, with science and Christian charity, if we are to be as one with the whole of God's universe. It is not theology in the ordinary religious sense. Pasternak's true quality is found in the wonderful strength of his sentient art. Like Lermontov, he is great in his passion and energy,—a lyric poet dedicated to his own conscience and his prophetic insight in the service of man. But like a wanderer returning home, in the steps of Pushkin he is great too in his compassion and magnanimity. Many have admired his spiritual strength, but few have grasped his essential loveliness exceeding strength. Bitter as his own life of desolation may have been, there appears in the pages of his final work a sense of lover's complaint, an air of meditative tenderness, simplicity, calm, and hope's abundance in the spiritual unity of all mankind.

EUGENE M. KAYDEN

MY SISTER LIFE

Summer of 1917

Dedicated to Lermontov

In Memory of The Demon

He came in the night
When the glacier shone blue, from Tamára.
His wings pointed out
Where nightmares hold sway, or fade.

He cried not, maligned not
The scourged, the naked, the bruised.
The gravestone still stands
By the fence near the Gruzian shrine.

Hunchbacked, grim,
The shadow was motionless under the grating.
The lute, by the lamp,
Was silent and shy about the princess.

Light sparkled in his hair;
It crackled like phosphor.
The colossus refused to hear
Why the Caucasus was greying for sorrow.

Not far from the windows,
While plucking his woolen burnoose,
He swore by the icy peaks:
Sleep, dearest! In an avalanche soon I return.

About My Verses

Along the pavement I will grind
A dust half sun, half glass. My deeds
In winter time the ceiling hears;
My verse the cold damp corner reads.

To window frames my garret room
Will bow, rehearsing verse, and prove
How folly, trouble, and adventure
Can, bursting, leapfrog to the roof.

The storm won't sweep across the moon,
But cover forms and ends estranged;
I'll suddenly remember suns
And find the world is long since changed.

Then Christmas like a crow will stare;
The boisterous day will playfully
Converse of matters unfamiliar
To my beloved and to me.

In a muffler, screwing up my eyes,
I'll shout to little boys at play
Below me in the yard: "My dears,
What millennium have we today?"

Who cleared a pathway to my door,
That hole all choked with sleet and snow,
While I was smoking with Lord Byron,
Drinking with Edgar Allan Poe?

Though long familiar, like Daryál,
I felt with Lermontov his truth—
The poet's hell, the poet's horror,
And soaked my life in his vermouth.

My Sister Life

My Sister—dear Life—in a downpour at dawn
Has flooded the world in a burst of spring;
But swaggering folk are puffed up and snappish;
Politely, politely, like vipers they sting.

The grownups, of course, will give you their reasons.
But your own, no doubt, are foolish, I'd say:
That eyes and lawns in a storm are lilac,
That horizons can smell like damp reseda.

In Maytime, no doubt, you attentively study
The time-table of trains at a local stage,
And it seems more impressive than holy scriptures
As your eyes drink in the enticing page.

There bevies of women from villages near
Crowd about the tracks in the sunset light,
While, impatient, I learn the stop is not mine.
Going down, the sun grieves with me in my plight.

The splash of the signalling bell swims off
With apologies still: Your station is far!
In the miles of night, downgrade, the fields
Disappear between carriage steps and a star.

My Sweet, my mirage, is asleep; folk drowse
In their houses, waking, and blinking again.
In the night, while splashing along the platforms,
My heart strews the carriage doors on the plain.

The Weeping Garden

The garden is frightful! It drips, it listens:
    Is it in loneliness here,
Crushing a branch like lace at a window,
    Or is there a witness near?

The earth is heavy with swollen burdens;
    Smothered, the spongy weald.
Listen! Afar, as though it were August,
    Night ripens in a field.

No sound. Not a stranger around to spy.
    Feeling deserted, alone,
It starts up again, dripping and tumbling
    On roof, gutter, flagstone.

I'll bring it close to my lips, and listen:
    Am I in loneliness here,
Ready to burst with tears in darkness,
    Or is there a witness near?

Deep silence. Not even a leaf is astir.
    No gleam of light to be seen.
Only choking sobs and the splash of slippers
    And sighs and tears between.

Dawnlight

In the breeze that asks the branches
If it's time for birds to sing,
Like a sparrow wet with raindrops,
O my lilac bloom, you swing!

The rain drips heavy buttons.
The garden, gleaming, peers
Bespattered and besprinkled,
Blue with a million tears.

My sorrow nursed the garden
All in thorns because of you;
Last night it lived in fragrance
And murmured sweet in dew.

It shook the panes and shutters
Nightlong in fretfulness;
A sudden bitter dampness
Passed lightly over your dress.

And roused by wondrous tidings
Of time and memories,
Today the morning gazes
With eyes like anemones.

Out of Superstition

A box of glazed sour fruit compact,
   My narrow room.
And oh the grime of lodging rooms
   This side the tomb!

This cubbyhole, out of superstition,
   I chose once more.
The walls seem dappled oaks; the door,
   A singing door.

You strove to leave; my hand was steady
   Upon the latch.
My forelock touched a wondrous forehead;
   My lips felt violets.

O Sweet! Your dress as on a day
   Not long ago
To April, like a snowdrop, chirps
   A gay "Hello!"

No vestal—you, I know: You came
   With a chair today,
Took down my life as from a shelf,
   And blew the dust away.

"Fresh Paint"

"Fresh paint." I should have read the sign.
  The Soul all fear defies,
And memory's stained with calves and cheeks,
  Hands, lips, and eyes.

But more than all good luck and sorrow
  You were to me most dear,
For white the yellow light became
  When you drew near.

I know, O dearest, my own gloom
  Will whiter be somehow,
Than fever whiter, or the lampshade,
  Or the bandage round my brow.

Patterns

O wretched *homo sapiens*
Entangled in his strife!
The few alone contrive
To live a gallant life.

The many, starved in mind,
Turn brutish, feel undone,
And miss the miracles
Of trees and air and sun.

O lily-scented hands!
O tender eyes in haze!
Night after night they set
My longing heart ablaze.

A cottage facing south
Beyond the village street
Gazed magically lone
In grass and meadow-sweet.

The canvas oil was dry;
The courting year was past,
Yet still her youth and braids
Lived flaming in my breast.

I again recall the fun
When swollen breezes blew
Our husks of sunflower seed
On burdock burrs in dew;

There, near the hollyhocks,
On every garden fence
I drew your smile and looks
In my youthful reverence.

And oft I came to splash
My canvas with fresh paint
While the laburnum grove
Received my ardent plaint.

And oft on trains to Moscow
I heard for stations back
The village ring-of-roses
Upon sleepers and the track;

The wells like balalaikas
Hummed long in dust a rune,
And ricks and poplar trees
Danced to a familiar tune.

Though pride may hurt the mind
And life tear hearts apart,
We'll brave our death, austere,
With striving in our hearts.

Swaying on a Bough

Swaying on a bough sweet-scented,
And drinking this blissfulness warm
In the dark, from chalice to chalice
A raindrop fell dazed by the storm.

And gliding from chalice to chalice,
It slid along two—a great tear
It hung, it sparkled in each,
An agate with trembling and fear.

The wind in the meadow blowing
May torture and flatten each drop,
But the pair will never be parted,
Or their kissing and drinking stop.

They sway and they laugh, trying
To be free, again to depart,
But the stamens hug them so tightly
That a knife won't cut them apart.

Resting Oars

The boat sways in my drowsy breast.
Low willows kiss my collarbone,
My elbows, oarlocks.—O let us rest!
Such joy waits here for everyone!

No matter! . . . Stay a little while. . . .
It means—with timid finger tips
To count the petals of camomile,
To crush the lilac with your lips!

It means—embrace the boundless skies,
Fold in your arms great Heracles!
It means—for nightingales and sighs
To squander all your wealth and ease!

Spring Rainstorm

The rain smiled at a birdcherry; drenched
The lacquer of cabs, the tremor of trees.
In moonlight, pop-eyed, the fiddlers filed
To the theatre.—Citizens, close your ranks!

Winds, pools of rain. As a throat choked
With tears, the innermost heart of roses
With jewels aflame! Rain, spout new joy
On roses, brows, eyelashes, clouds!

The moon silvers their fluttering dresses,
Linked arms, the triumph of jubilant lips,
And shapes in plaster their epic, shapes
A bust no hand has modelled in life.

Whose blood, in passion, suddenly flooded
The heart to the brim with hope and glory?
Behold, a leader's hand has gripped
Lips and aortas tight in its steel.

Not rain nor night nor multitudes striving
Together, shouting hurrahs to Kerensky,
But a blinding escape from catacombs
And last despairs, to the open, unto light.

No roses, lips, or the roar of throats,
No rage of crowds in blind commotion,
But the swelling tides of Europe's unrest
In a storm exultant on asphalt squares.

Stars in Summertime

They talk some awful things
And give the right address.
They peer around, inquire;
They move as upon a stage.

O silence! You're the fairest
Of everything I've known!
Some feel it is outrageous
That mice have wings to fly.

In July the village nights
Are marvelously white;
Deep skies provide a chance
For pranks and hurt and harm.

They splash their glitter round
And flash their gaiety,—
At a precise degree,
At a right meridian.

The breezes try to raise
A rose at the request
Of laughing lips and locks,
Of hems and dear nicknames.

They bubble over, warm
With laughter, and they scorn
The grownups' solemn saws
And fumbling idle tales.

An English Lesson

When Desdemona came a-singing,
And a little time to live had she—
Not love, her fatal star, she sobbed:
It was a willow, willow tree.

When Desdemona came a-singing,
With firmer voice and lifted head,
Her demon at her death prepared
A psalm of a weeping river bed.

And when Ophelia came a-singing,
And a little time to live had she—
Like storms that sweep a hayloft clean
Her soul was swept of misery.

And when Ophelia came a-singing,
Sick with bitter dreams and grief,
What trophies in her grave had she?
Sweet celandine and willow leaf.

Their passions fell away like rags,
And silent into the pool of night
And time they went, with aching hearts,
Their loving forms transfused in light.

Definition of Poetry

It's a summons sternly swelling,
The cracking of shattered icicles,
The night that blasts young leaves,
The contest of two nightingales,

The stifled sweet pea on the vine,
The cry of a world at birth,
Figaro from flutes and the platform
In a crashing fall among rose beds.

It's all that night will reveal
In the steep depths of a pool—
To carry a star to the lake
Alone in its trembling wet arms.

Like dank wood, the stifling air,
When the sky is choked by alders;
Gay stars could rock with laughter
At blockheads sunk flat in mud.

Definition of the Soul

To fall off, a ripe pear in a storm,
With one leaf in loyalty bound.
O blind faith! To abandon the branch,
To choke in dry dust on the ground!

To fall, more aslant than the wind.
O blind faith: "I'm safe!" In a flash
Of glory it died in the storm,
And darkly is crumbled in ash.

My country's ablaze in the storm.
Say, fledgling, where now your nest?
O my leaf, like a goldfinch in fear!
Why struggle, O shyest and best?

And whither, in fear, do you strive,
O my song, in parting from me?
Ah, the mortal "stay here" we despised
When together we throbbed on the tree.

Definition of Creative Art

With shirt wide open at the collar,
Maned as Beethoven's bust, it stands;
Our conscience, dreams, the night and love,
Are as chessmen covered by its hands.

And one black king upon the board:
In sadness and in rage, forthright
It brings the day of doom.—Against
The pawn it brings the mounted knight.

In gardens where from icy spheres
The stars lean tender, linger near,
Tristan still sings, like a nightingale
On Isolde's vine, with trembling fear.

The gardens, ponds, and fences, made pure
By burning tears, and the whole great span,
Creation—are only bursts of passion
Hoarded in the hearts of men.

Our Thunderstorm

The storm, like a priest, burns the lilac
And dims with sacrificial smoke
Both eyes and clouds.—How shall one heal
With lips alone the ant's crushed limb?

The clank of pails knocked all askew!
What greed! The sky's not large enough?
A hundred hearts throb in a ditch.
The storm, like a priest, burns the lilac.

The meadow gleams, enamel. Like ice,
The earth's scraped clean of azure hues.
But, look, the finches do not hasten
To quit their life of ecstasy!

They sip from tubs the passing storm,—
The sweet, from nature's gift of plenty.
The clover's purple and deep brown
In painters' splash of claret light.

Mosquitoes cling to raspberries.
But the malarial proboscis
Stings in a frenzy, savage-like,
Where summer splendor glows its best:

It leaves an abscess under a blouse,
Then, like a ballerina, leaps away
To plunge headlong its insolence
Where blood is moist as leaves in dew.

Oh, trust my sportive play! Believe
That migraine roaring in your wake,
Like wrathful day whose fate's to burn,
Like wilding blooms on birdcherry trees.

You do believe me?—Closer, dear!
Bring close your face again! I'll fan
Your sacred summer radiance
And make it flame for you and me.

I shan't keep back my all from you.
You hide your lips in jasmine snow.
I feel that snow on my lips too,—
How sweet it melts in dearest dreams!

What shall I do with all my joy?
Hide it away in lines of verse?
Their lips by now are wholly cracked
From poisons on the printed page.

They war against the alphabet,
Blaze red confusion in your cheeks.

Sparrow Hills

My kisses across your breast, like water from a jug!
They'll have an end, and soon, our days of summer heat.
Nor shall we every night rise up in trailing dust
The hurdy-gurdy's bellow, stamp and drag our feet.

I've heard about old age. What ominous forebodings!
That no wave will lift again to the stars its hands,
That waters will speak no more; no god in the woods;
No heart within the pools; no life in meadowlands.

O rouse your soul! This frenzied day is yours to have!
It is the world's midday. Why don't you use your eyes?
Look, there's thought upon high hills in seething bubbles
Of heat, woodpeckers, cones and needles, clouds and skies.

Here tracks of city trolleys stop, and further
The pines alone must satisfy. Trams cannot pass.
It is always Sunday there! Plucking little branches,
There the clearing capers, slipping on the grass.

And strewing sunrays, Whitsun, and rambling walks,
The woods will have us say the world was always so:
Conceived like that by forests, hinted to the meadows,
And spilt by clouds as on a chintz design below.

Disagreement

Arrow hands race down the walls.
The hours are beetles in the grasses.
Stop, why hurl the plates about,
Sound the alarm, smash the glasses?

Even in this country cottage
Things can't shape themselves like that.
Who in love is lucky—always?
Do not fear the thunderclap!

It may strike, and flare like a wet
Cabin charged by a lightning ring.
Then they'll give away the puppies.
Rain-blown shots will pierce the wing.

Let the forest be our hallway
Warm in moonlight. Life is fair!
Trouble's like a new-washed apron
Hung to dry in lisping air.

And if waterspouts of sadness
Drive you forth, the storms will roar.
Storms will praise your well-kept house:
Can you really ask for more?

As a gnat inside an oil lamp
So one year has burned away.
See, he got up wet and sleepy
In the grey-blue dawn of day.

See, he's peering through the window
Dread with pity, old with fears.
See, his pillow's wet with crying
Where he buried deep his tears.

What will please that ragged body?
Look, he cannot jest in gladness!
What in the empty summer days
Will relieve his stifling sadness?

Woods are veiled with leaden fringes,
And the burdock's sad and grey.
Let him weep. But you are lovely,
All in eagerness, like day!

Why's that numskull crying? Can he
Feel the lovers' heart of trust?
Are, then, sunflowers in the village
Dimmed, like suns, by rain and dust?

Sultry Night

A drizzle fell. It did not bend
The grasses in the thunder's track.
Dust swallowed up the pills of raindrops
Like iron powdered soft and black.

The village hoped for no salvation,
And low the poppy, swooning, waved;
Inflamed, the standing rye grew red,
Defiled—a god that raved.

Throughout the orphaned, sleepless, vast,
Sick meadowlands in open spaces
The storms lay dying, still, and wails
Flew headlong from the dwelling places.

Close after them came blindly fleeing
A scant few drops. Beside the fence,
Between wet branches and the wind,
A quarrel arose. My heart grew tense.

They spoke of me. I felt the garden
Would chatter, fearful, long, in heat.
But in the talk of bush and shutters
I went unnoticed from the street.

If they see me here, I can't go back:
They'll chatter, chatter, to the end.

A Still More Sultry Dawn

All morning long the pigeon cooed
At your window.
In water troughs
Like sleeves of dampened shirts
Lay branches, dying.
A drizzle fell. Small clouds
Came lightly through a dusty market place,
Lulling my sadness,
So I feared,
Upon a hawker's tray.
I prayed they'd stop in flight.
I thought they would.
Dawn came ashen, as the talk of prison mates,
As a squabble stirred among the bushes.

I prayed the hour would come
When behind your windows,
Your water-basin, like a mountain ice-drift
Would roar
With scraps of broken song,
And cheek and forehead warm from sleep
Would glow as ice within a burning glass
Upon your dressing table.
But the spheres because of talk
Beneath the banner of the scudding clouds
Did not hear the prayer
I murmured in snow-powdered silence,
Drenched like an overcoat,
Like dusty sounds of busy threshing,
Like a loud squabble among the bushes.

I begged them:
Stop your torture;
Let me sleep!—
A mist rose up, and tramping,
The clouds passed through the dusty market
Like recruits plodding their way to fields.
They trudged in endless time,
Like captive Austrians,
Like silence moaning,
Ever moaning:
"A drink of water,
Please!"

Moochkap

My heart is stifled; the horizon's like
My thoughts—dirt-brown inferior
Tobacco. These windmills bring to mind
A seashore, grey sails, a sloop of war.

They loom like stiffened sails along
A winged anchorage in the still air;
All mute they seem with frenzied anguish,
With stark impatience and despair.

And, oh, the hour slips, like a pebble
In shallows ricocheting, down
The bay. Not sinking, no! It's there
Like my thoughts—tobacco, faded brown.

Then shall I see her soon? One hour
Of waiting here before her train,
One hour gripped tight by apathy
Of hellish dark and storm again.

Home At Last

Sultry heat on seven hills;
Flocks of doves in mildewed hay.
From the sun the turban slips:
Time to pull up from the pail
A wet towel into the air
And wrap it round the cupolas.

Streets astir with vocal chords,
Shuffling wenches and rosebeds.

Draw the window-curtains close;
Shut the stamp of strollers out.
What an opiate this life!
Sheer insomnia—the kiss!

Sweaty, dirty from a journey,
The city stumbles into bed.
Now at last a clean fresh breeze
From a far-off steppe blows in.
Stifled cries and curses hang
Long in moveless space. . . .
Bridges, signs! A night of stars!
Oh, to sleep again! . . .

Summer 1917

Athirst for moths and butterflies
And stains the summer waited;
About us the woven memories
Of heat and mint and honey.

No chime of clocks but ringing flails
From dawn to evening dusk,
Stinging the air with panting dreams
Enravished by the weather.

Sometimes the gladsome sunset, idling,
Surrendered to cicadas
And stars and trees its governance
Of kitchens and of gardens.

The moon spread long uneven beams
Or hid itself in dark;
And softly, softly flowed the night
From cloud to passing cloud.

Not like a shower, but in a dream,
In shy forgetfulness,
The small rain shuffled at the door
With the smell of winecorks in the air.

The smell in dust, the smell in grass.
And if one cared to learn,
The smell of gentry copybooks
Was all of rights and brotherhood.

The councils met in the villages;
You, at their meetings, too?
The days hung bright like sorrel,
The smell of winecorks in the air.

Summer Thunderstorm

Then Summer said goodbye
To the station. Tipping his cap,
The thunder took as souvenirs
A hundred blinding snaps.

The lilac darkened. With armfuls
Of lightning, plucked in the night,
He flooded from the meadows
The overseer's house with light.

And when a wave of malice
The roof had overflowed,
And like charcoal on a drawing
Rains rushed in a solid flood,

The crumbling sense began to blink:
It seemed, though bright and gay,
The mind in its remotest corners
Would be lighted clear as day.

Darling, It Frightens Me!

Darling, it frightens me! A poet
In love loves like a pagan god.
Chaos then creeps to light again
As when the world was first begot.

His eyes weep tons of mist. Shrouded
In clouds, he seems of mammoth size.
He's out of date. Our times are new:
He's not in step, not civilized!

He sees how people wed, get drunk,
Then sleep it off, and how the spawn
Of swampy frogs, by marriage rites,
Becomes the best caviar in town.

They squeeze the gift of life, this pearl
By a Watteau, into a narrow box.
They hate the man who shows them up
For the vain and coward weathercocks

They are. They cringe; they lie like drones.
They mock because from common clay
He lifts a woman up in her worth,
A bacchante from her amphora.

The dawn of day burns in his breath,
Andean peaks, by the sign and power
Of starry dust, while village nights
Reel, bleating, paler every hour.

Today the reek of ancient gullies,
Each murky fecund vestry-room,
Like a mattress-bed of typhoid pain,
Festers in its jungle gloom.

Let's Strew Our Words

Let's strew our words about
As gardens—bark and amber,
All but, all but regardless,
And, yes, all but free-handed.

No need to start debating
With grand formality
Why leaves with lemon gleam
And with madder flash in dew;

Why needles shine with tears,
Or who it was who crashed
Through bars of window-blinds
To shelves of music notebooks;

Who smeared with rowan berry
The rug behind the door
With fair transparent tow
And shimmering italics.

You ask who still ordains,
Makes August glow, who knows
That every trifle matters?
Or whose uncommon care

Forms every maple leaf?
Who since Ecclesiast days
Has fashioned at his post
The alabaster stone?

You ask who still ordains
That September lips of dahlia
And aster bloom should suffer?
That the small leaves of broom
From gray caryatides
Alight on wet flagstones
Near autumn hospitals?

You ask who still ordains? ...
The Almighty God of love,
The Almighty of details,—
Of Yagáilo and Yadvíga!

I cannot solve the riddle
Of what's beyond the grave;
But life, like Autumn silence,
Is rich in all details.

Postscript

No, I am not the cause of your sorrow.
It was not for me you left your country.
It was the sunlight aflame on drops of ink
As on clusters of dusty currants.

In the veins of my thoughts and letters
Cochineal appeared.
That purple was not of my making.
No, I am not the cause of your sorrow.

It was evening, moulded of dust, when panting,
I kissed you, smothered by your ochre, pollen.
It was the shadows feeling your pulse.
By the fences you opened your face to the plains;
You flamed in the air and the varnish of gates
Flooded by twilight, poppy, and ash.

It was summertime glowing in labels
Alongside the pools, like bags in the heat of the sun,
That stamped the boatman's chest as with wax,
That scorched your dresses and hats.

It was your lashes closed from the sunshine;
It was the sun, untamed, that had polished its horns
On the fences, butting and smashing stockades.
It was the west in your hair like a ruby
That buzzed and slowly died
Into purple and raspberry red.
No, not I, but you—all your beauty I loved.

THEMES AND VARIATIONS

Encounter

Nightlong and through the early morning,
Since six o'clock, since four, since two,
Water rushed out of pipes and holes
And pools, off fences, wind, and roofs.

The walks grew slippery, the winds
Had ripped the water like gunny sack,
And one could go as far as Podolsk
And nowhere meet a soul abroad.

At six o'clock, in a break of landscape,
From a stairway sodden with the damp,
A weary "See you then tomorrow"
Split off and plunged into the water.

Somewhere with automatic pulleys
And rattling chains, anticipating
A day of water-drains, the East
Mechanically worked her spell.

Tricked out in frowzy finery,
Horizons drowsed above frosted kvass,
And coughed, and loudly shouted after
Their heady bouillabaisse of March.

The author and the March Night came
Together, still arguing, side by side,
Led homeward by the chilly landscape—
The pair led home from a meeting place.

The March Night and the author walked
In a hurry home, but spied from time
To time a phantom flashing past them,
Or vanishing before their eyes.

The dawn! As at an amphitheater,
When people heed the precursor's call,
The Tomorrow on the steps proclaimed
Rushed, fluttering, to meet the pair.

It came like a joiner with his frame:
Then houses, trees, and temples seemed
As lost, as alien in this world,
In the frame's unattainable expanse.

The pair soon spoke in hexameters.
They slipped to right across the frame.
But trimmers were dragged off for dead,
And no one ever marked their loss.

1922

Mephistopheles

On Sundays from beyond the turnpike
And piled-up dust, they trooped pellmell,
While showers, finding them away
From home, burst in their bedroom windows.

At dinner time it was their custom
To serve some scanty shares of rain,
While the whirlwind darted on its wheel
Around the cupboards in the room.

And while the silken window blinds
At home rolled straightway to the ceiling,
The ponds, the flowers, the open air
Shoved hard the crowd of dolts and oafs.

Later long lines of carriages
Drew together around the city wall
Where a shadow, scaring all the horses,
Every night came suddenly alive.

In blood-red stockings held by ribbons
His fiendish legs, like tracking straps
Hung from a drum, kicked up the dust
On highways drenched in sunset rays.

It seemed that, whirled up in a stream
Of arrogance from overhanging leaves,
The sun's disdain would level worlds,
But put up only with these feathers.

He looked on folk as only signposts,
And scarcely touched his hat in greeting;
He strode on, shaking loud with laughter,
And, merry, hugged his friend alone.

1919

Shakespeare

A coaching yard, and, looming over the river
In terraces, the gloomy Tower set back.
The clanking of hoofs and the rheumy pealing
Of Westminster, from muffled piles in black.

The narrow streets. The reeking houses, crowded,
That hoard the damp in their branching timbers,
Morose from soot and sodden from ale;
And crooked lanes by London cold enshrouded.

The snow falls sluggishly in darkness.
It came tumbling at twilight, wrinkled somewhat,
Half drowsy, like a crumpling belly band,
And smothered each deserted sleepy lot.

A small window, with bits of violet mica
In leaden rims. . . . "Damn this weather!
We may sleep in the cold, in the open yet.
Now on to a barrel! Hey, barber, water!"

As he shaves, he cackles, holding his sides
At the wit of a jester jabbering since dinner
And straining through a pipe stuck to his lips
His tedious trifles.
     But Shakespeare bides,
Impatient with jesting and bored by the saws.
The sonnet he wrote with not one blot,
At white heat, last night at that far table
Where curdled rennet laps at lobster claws—

The sonnet speaks to him:
                              "Sir, I acclaim
Your talents, but, O my poet and master,
Do you know—you and that dolt astride
That barrel there with soap on his mug,
I'm swifter than lightning, nobler by nature
Than mortals? In brief, that, scourged in my flame,
You begin to stink like your foul tobacco?

"Forgive me, old man, my filial skepticism,
But, Sir, my good lord, I believe we lie
At an inn. Are your cronies my kind? Your verse,
For the mob? Sir, grant me the infinite sky!

"Well, read it to him! Why not? In the name
Of all guilds and bills—in his company—
Five yards away—at billiards with him,
Do you like this sort of popularity?"

"Read to him? Are you mad?" He calls for the waiter.
And fiddling with a bunch of Malaga grapes,
He reckons: half pint, French stew. And he runs,
Flinging his napkin at the phantom shape.

1919

A Theme with Variations

You have never felt
The eyes of Egypt's ancient statues,
Their calm, unmoving, silent gaze,
And glory of uplifted heads. . . .
You have never felt the hidden tie
Between the sphinxes and our fate.
A. GRIGÓRYEV

The Theme

A crag. A storm. A crag, cocked hat, and cape.
A crag—and Pushkin, the man who to this day,
Through shuttered eyes, erect, sees in the Sphinx
Not our own puzzled views and cant, nor wild
Surmises that had baffled the Greek mind
But his ancestor, thick-lipped son of Ham,
Whose wrinkled face bore to our distant plains,
Like pox, the face of pitted desert sands.
All this and nothing more. A crag. A storm.

The fury of froth-lashing tumbling beer
From lips of crag and cliff and scarps of hills,
And holes and hollows. And the roar of seas
Beneath the water-spouting moon, churned up
In caverned vats. Fierce gales and sucking pools.
The burst of light and flare of dazzling foam
Grip fast his watchful eyes alert in storms.
The breakers spare no candle-flames against
The Sphinx, and surge with darting flames again.

44

A crag. A storm. A crag, cocked hat, and cape.
Across the Sphinx's lips the salt sea scent
And driven mist. The sands all round are slush
With humid kisses of Medusan maids.

He pays no heed to scales of siren shapes:
How could he take fish-tails for truth who once
Had used a chalice hollowed of their bones
With glinting stars like beams of light on ice?

A crag. A storm. From haughty glances hidden,
A child's gay laughter—oh so strange and soft—
At play with ancient desert bones long after
Psammetichus was king. . . .

1. Original Variation

Above festive high cliffs and the sea,
The violent storms of Trebizónd
In their flight with froth on their lips,—
With docks and the clatter of anchors

And shipwrecks flung up and the swollen
Drowned bodies of seamen and battered
Grey hulls in harbor,—are stifled
In the breakers of Pilsen-like spray.

There, toppling from high mountain walls,
The fountains and rocks in their fear
Call loud with an earthquake of sound;
There phosphates blister the land;

There the crystal frenzy of surges
And the thunder of storms are sucked in
Like beer, like betel-nut leaves,
By the shifting shingles and sands:

Are the storms an African birthright?
How much, the Imperial Lycée?—
Twin gods for a day embattled,
Twin seas by conflict transformed.

Free primitive passion linked with
The freedom of passion in verse.
Twin days of two separate worlds;
Twin dramas of two ancient acts.

2. *Derivative Variation*

"He stood upon a lonely shore
Grave with his lofty thoughts of State."
The sea ran high, and, stiff with sand,
The blood-red waters were in flood.
There, like the surging sea in wrath,
Pushkin stood fierce in his revolt,
In anger, troubled in his heart.

Tomorrow lived upon his lips
As others lived with *yesterdays*.
The fever of the days to come
Leaped wild in his imagination,
And the future as a mist caressed
The heavy lashes of his eyes.
The pages of his dream sank slow,
Engulfed in time. As in a mist
He felt the story of his life,—
An event no climate could bring forth,
No desert heat could dissipate
In fact, no storm could bring about,
No Maytime dawn or August noon
Could scatter ever to the winds.

The land lay wild, unendingly
Beyond the cliff. Where white-maned crests
Curved sharp about the bathing-place,
Wind-cloven billows in the reefs
Hovered like spinning water spires
A frenzied second in the air,

And toppled down in screeching blasts,
To cease in caverns of the deep.
Too wild the sector of the world
Beyond the cliff, too violent
The insurmountable great hand
Which spilled abroad the briny nectar
On sightless rigging lost in space,
As day after day drifted past
In twilight cold, on anguished waves,
Unpitied in the murky night.—
O savage, free, and stern the scene
Of strife and wonder and delight!

He clambered down. The rude, wild wind
Thundered from crag to gulf, and churned
The waves to froth. The wormwood, broom,
And golden gorge clutched at his cane
And grieved his weary path, and fierce
The whirlwinds from the distant steppes.
The frothy margins of the shore
Sent shudders through the irises
And reeds; they rippled end to end
In eddies toward the lilac center
Of gloaming and unclouded pools.
The ripples mocked, as though a sportsman's
Sinker slid smoothly downward, sank,
And rested, slithering, in silt,
And nodded that inscrutable
Grimace by which the float mocks at
The baffled rod, without a word,
"Poor fishing here; I told you so!"

He sank upon a rock, and not
A feature showed his agitation,
His straining at long last to read
The gospel of the ocean depths.

The smallest seaside shell treasures
Its rustling heart, its secret dream,
Which lives as fettered by some grief
And great unease. No knife will prize
The valves apart, and learn the ache
And secret of the loving heart,
Or hear the joyous sob of life
That builds the underwater reef,
Stains red the coral lips, expires
As a text in the sea's anemone.

3. The Racing Stars

The racing stars. The wash of seas on a shore.
The salt spray blinded. And tears grew dry.
Bedrooms in darkness brooded. Racing thoughts.
The Sphinx in stillness watched the Sahara sky.

The candles flared. It seemed the blood froze
In the huge Colossus. Lips smiled inside
The swelling blue smile of the wilderness.
Night faded with the ebbing of the tide.

A breeze from far Morocco stirred the sea.
The simoom blew. Archangel snored in snows.
The candles flared. The first draft of *The Prophet*
Lay dry. And morning on the Ganges rose.

4. Clouds. And Stars.

Clouds. And stars. The road.
Aléko—aloof—a misfit.
Moons of Zemfíra's eyes
Glow—a bottomless pit.

Shafts flung up to the sky.
Faces bronzed and bold.
Gipsies squint at starry
Necklaces of gold.

Camps like Chaldean roofs
Under the moon's cold blaze.
Blood runs cold.—Jealous?
Jealousy never pays.

Halt, you Syrian eunuch!
Chasing a star ablaze?
Crazed by plans of revenge?
Murder?—It never pays.

Shadows like eunuchs stay,
Hang about open ways.
Poison?—Storms of anger:
Suicide never pays.

Leap! Swelled out nostrils.
Still, unappeased, in a daze?
Steady!—They'll guess, surmise.
Flight?—It never pays.

5. Gypsy Splendor

He comprehended gypsy splendor.
Sick from the scurvy, he attained
The lessons of the reedy pipe
Among wine-bibbers, footpads, thieves.

Freebooters by dark fences crept;
The vineyards hid behind sun tan;
The sparrows at the clusters pecked
And scarecrows shook, aghast in tatters.
Winds boded trouble in the clusters
And, rustling, in the vineyards died.

Death-flaming seas. The thunders crashed
Against the shores, and shingles rattled.
The rocks spewed, answering the gale,
And surges pitched their muddy froth.

The stormwind roared beyond Shabú
And toppled trembling mooring-blocks.
Brine-soaked in spouting, retching surfs,
The cordage grew hard in the squall.

Like squabbling gullies in a storm,
Like bawling, booming bath-houses,
Kagúl kept chattering all night
With jabbering Ochákov gulls.

6. The Sunset Steppe

The sunset steppe grew chill and dark.
Like night, a pensive grasshopper
Gave ear to distant clink of bridles
And jingling bells and ringing voices.

Then drowsily the steppe at times
Stirred up a hobbled sleepy breeze,
Just like a loosened bridle-bit
Or trailing chain along the ground.

The motley tatters faded far,
And, chilled, as brasses of some scales,
Immeasurably blue in space
The boundless South turned up its face—
To jabber, whistle, trill carefree,
That man might long and sigh again
In wonder at unspotted skies,
In wonder neath a night of stars.

A moment slipped—to feel and see,
And yet it eclipsed eterniy.

1918

That May Happen
(*from* MALADY: 3)

That may happen one way or another,
At a certain fateful hour
When, gagging you, blacker than monks and clergy
Insanity may get you down.

Frost. The night outside the window watches,
As is its custom, the firming ice.
Inside its fur coat, sunk in that armchair,
The Soul is purring on and on the same old tune.

Its cheek, the profile of a bough,
The poker's shadow, and the parquet floor,
Mould out of remorse and dreaming
The guilty blizzard raging long for days.

The night is still. The night is clear and frosty.
Like a blind puppy lapping milk
The palings drink the starlight among
Fir trees deep in unfathomable gloom.

Perhaps the fir trees gleam, perhaps they drip,
Perhaps a taper's flaring in the night.
The snow blinds fir after fir beneath its paws;
The trees are silhouetted against other trees.

Perhaps the silence, perhaps the sky,
Or the elegy of telegraphic waves,
Was a longing for the cry of "Answer!"
Or was it the echo of another silence?

Perhaps no hearing lives in twigs and needles,
No hearing in the silence of the spheres;
Perhaps the gleam's the answer within the ether
To someone's lingering "Hullo!"

Frost. The night outside the window watches,
As is its custom, the firming ice.
Inside its fur coat, sunk in that armchair,
The Soul is purring on and on the same old tune.

Oh, his lips! He bites them till they bleed.
He's trembling; his face is in his hands.
For his biographer that chalklike face
And gestures portend a storm of speculation.

1919

January 1919
(*from* MALADY: 7)

That year! How often by the window
The old year muttered: "Well, jump out!"
But with a Christmas tale of Dickens
The new year puts despondency to rout.

He whispers: "Shake it off. Forget!"
He strives with the rising sun outside.
The old year talked to me of strychnine,
Or fell to vials of cyanide.

Our peace he scoops up with his dawn,
His hands, his idly streaming locks of hair—
Our peace from roofs and birds outside,
A peace well known to philosophers.

He came; he stretched himself in light
From panels, himself in service to the snow.
He's insolent, beside himself;
He shouts, he calls for drinks, he makes a show,

He's wild and rowdy! He brings with him
The vulgar street! What can we do?—Be sure,
There's not a grief in all the world
So great the snows of winter will not cure.

1919

Lovers' Quarrel

1. O Treacherous Angel

O treacherous angel, I should have curbed
Your insatiate thirst with my nectar of sorrow!
I am as I am: why claim a tooth for a tooth?
O the hurt and the lies begot from the start!
O the festering grief in the end!

O treacherous angel, no, not fatal
This pain, this eczema of my suffering heart.
But why inflict as a gift, at parting,
Corruption, yes, sickness? Why your trifling,
Your rainfall of kisses? Why, in public,
For spite, do you knowingly mock me in scorn?

2. O the Shame!

O the shame! the sorrow I bear! In this break
And quarrel, how many illusions may still endure!
Were I only a heap of matter scraped together
Of hands, lips, brows, shoulders, cheeks, eyes!—

I'd yield my youthful ardor and eagerness
And strength to the cry of my lines and cruel words:
I'd lead them bold to the attack, outflank,
And storm your citadel, the cause of my disgrace.

3. I'll Free Myself

I'll free myself, in my thoughts from you,
If not at parties, drinking, in heaven then!
The neighbors, at a ring, will answer
To a stranger—let someone in, some time.

I'll burst upon them—in gay December.
A knock, and quick I'll be in the hall:
"You're come from there? What are they saying?
What's new? What gossip goes on in the city?"

Is all my anguish in vain?
Will it whisper at all, "She seemed like stone"
And leap, on the run, with a battering question,
With a cry of surprise, "You—really you?"

And shall I be spared in public squares?
If you could but feel my longing and pain
When, a hundred times a day, the streets
Reflect your likeness as they stare, amazed!

4. Stop Me If You Dare!

Stop me if you dare! Do your best to quench this flame,
This violent fit of sadness that rattles and soars
Like mercury in a Torricelli tube!
Come hinder me, vanquish my madness, tell me to stop!
Restrain me from raving about you! . . . Why be ashamed?
Smother me, kiss me again, again!

5. Entwine This Shower

Entwine this shower, like a wave of cool elbows,
Like lilies all satin and strong, with languid hands!
To the fields! Rejoice! Lay hold! In this boisterous race
The woods are resounding with echoes of hunts in Calydon,
Where Actaeon rashly pursued Atalanta, like a roe;
Where they kissed in the glade, in infinite azure
That whistled by the ears of the horses;
Where they kissed in the passionate baying of the chase,
In the pealing of horns, and the cracking of trees,
And the noise of hoofs and claws.
To the fields! Come, free! To the fields!

6. Disillusioned?

Disillusioned? Then you think it is best
In a swan-song requiem for us to part?
With a show of sorrow, sullen, with tears
In your widening eyes, to win meekly by art?

As if frescoes could crumble and crack
In compassion Sebastian's lips! I hate,
From tonight, for I see the dallying fool
In myself, and regret that I haven't a whip.

All in dark, unheeding, you quickly resolve
To plough everything up, without fail,
Regardless. Like Time.— Suicide? Why that?
It's slow, too slow,—the pace of a snail.

7. My Darling, Dearest!

My darling, dearest! As the night from Bergen to the Pole
Falls off the loons' hot down in racing snowstorms,
So here I swear, my Sweet, I swear and mean it truly
When I beg you, darling, please forget.—Sleep.

When, like a whaling hulk ice-jammed to the very funnels,
A winter's phantom stiffened to the masts with ice, I seem
A fool in your terror-stricken eyes, be calm, and sleep:
'Twill heal before you're wed, my darling. Do not weep.

For like the arctic North that secretly, unknown
To wakeful icebergs beyond familiar places, will rinse
The eyes of blinded seals under a midnight dome of light,
I beg you, dry your eyes. Don't worry now: Sleep.

8. My Table's Not Wide Enough

My table's not wide enough to bear my weight
Across the board, to let me crook my elbows
And hide for long the isthmus of my anguish—
Past miles of waste that word 'forgive' has scarred.

(It is night there now) Ah, to have your sultry hair,
(They've gone to sleep) your shoulders, realm of arms!
(All the lights are out). I'd take them back at dawn,
And the porch would greet them with a drowsy branch.

O hide me with your hands, warm hands alone,
With kind tormenting fingers, ten, in rifts of
Baptismal stars, like semaphores that point
Late trains northbound again in whirling snows!

9. The Trembling Piano

The trembling piano licks the foam from its lips.
This frenzy will crack your heart. "Dearest,"
You whisper. "No!" I shout back to you. "Never!
While playing music?"—And yet we are nearest

In twilight here, the music tossed upon
The fire, year after year, like a diary.
O wondrous memories that beckon still,
That strike the spirit dumb! Look, you are free!

I do not hold you. Go. Do good to others.
Go quickly now. Enough of *Werther's* pain.
But in our time the air's defiled with death:
To open a window is like opening a vein.

1918

You Think I Could Forget?

You think I could forget—my own,
The sea? Ride trains by plan and map?
Flinch at party men, from my ordeals?
Emotion-drugged, fall in a trap?

Or ride first-class, in a dining car?
Mark stations, lovely spots, and spas? . . .
Rain blows! I'm proud of all my scars!
I know you, tigers, by your claws!

My own, the sea! I've known the farce
Of empty days, the pangs and rue
Harsher than prison woes. . . . Rain blows!
'Tis I, the proletarian,—not you!

How low I sank! Chastise me: I sank
To the apathy of beasts of late.
I abased myself—and you, my Love,
Who grieve for me, disconsolate.

1921

Thus Life Begins

Thus life begins: When two years old,
They live in light and melody;
They chirp, they babble. Then the gold
Of words they find when they are three.

And thus they learn to understand.
But in the din of turbines whirled
About, their land seems not their land,
Their humble home a foreign world.

What trouble broods that menacing
Wild beauty—there by the lilac tree—
If to steal children's not the thing?
Thus fear will breed anxiety

And greater fears. Can one endure
A star, who feels one's bound to win,
Like Faust, although a dreamer pure
And simple? Thus gypsy ways begin.

Then soaring over huts and trees
And yards where folk should feel at home,
They glimpse some undiscovered seas.
And thus iambic verses come.

Thus summer nights will, kneeling, pray
In wheaten fields *Thy will be done*,
Yet menace through your eyes the Day.
They pick a quarrel with the Sun.

Thus verses set them on their way.

1919

63

We Are Few

We are few. Perhaps three: a dark
Infernal lot, embittered, wet
Beneath a grey and racing bark
Of rains, low clouds—the soviet
Of soldiers, of debates and curses,
Disputes about fares and verses.

We were people. An epoch now,
We are swept on caravan trails
As the tundra's swept in the sough
Of pistons, tender, and rails.
We swoop, break through, interpose,
We swirl,—a whirlwind of crows.

You'll not understand until late.
When winds in the morning confound
The thatch of the roofs, a debate
In the congress of trees will resound,
Astir with immortal speech
Where the shingled roofs do not reach.

1921

My Pictures Swing

My pictures swing in the thundershower
With a wind that blows my candles out,
And I cannot stop their swinging rhyme,
Their flight from walls and hooks about.

Suppose the world is behind a mask,
Against the mind's free play? Suppose,
That some will dare to cement its mouth,
And seal it against the winter snows?

Besides, things fling all masks away,
Despite convention, honor, power,
If there is good reason for a song,
If there is the season for a shower.

1922

In the Wood

The wood is swirling with cathedral darkness,
And heavy with lilac heat the meadow glares.
What's left to them—for secrecy and kissing?
Like wax in eager hands, the world is theirs.

Such is the changeless dream: You do not sleep,
But dream you long for sleep, that someone lies
In dreaming near, that underneath his eyelids
Two suns sear black the lashes of his eyes.

The sunlight ebbs. The iridescent beetles.
The glass of dragonflies and wings ablaze
Across his cheeks. The woodland gleams like gems
In a watchmaker's hands, alert with sunset rays.

It seems he slumbers to the tick of numbers,
While in the amber sky the spirits place
A regulated clock within the ether
As if to gauge the change of heat in space.

They shift the clock about, shake pine-needles,
Strew shadows, nettles; they swing and bore into
The day's fatigue a swelling mast of shadows
Upon the clock-face shimmering in blue.

It seems, as leaves, as light, their bliss is old;
It seems the woodland holds their sunset dreams.
But happy people do not watch the clock.
They only sleep, those two, or so it seems.

1917

66

The House at Spásskoye

This memorable September's strewn about Spásskoye.
Is today not the time for your leaving the villa?
Beyond fences the Echo replied to the herdsman,
Rang out in the woods to the stroke of the axe.

The marshes shivered near the park last night.
The sun reappeared, then quickly went down.
No harebell will drink of rheumatic dews;
Now the lilac dropsy has smutted the birches.

Disconsolate woods. They are longing for rest
Under snows, the unwaking slumber of bear dens.
The trees among stumps, inside blackened fences,
Gape like an obituary within a black border.

More faded and spotted the birchwood each day,
Still thinner and duller its watery shade.
Moreover, it grumbles: You are now fifteen,
But what, O my child, shall we do with them?

There are many, I'd say—no matter for jesting—
Like mushrooms by hedges, like birds in a bush.
We've shrouded our own horizon with them
And veiled other views of life with their mists.

On his deathbed the typhus-feverish clown
Hears the gallery's roar of Homeric laughter.
The same anguish beholds, in hallucination,
From the highway now this timbered old house.

1918

So Be It

The dawn swings wild the candlelight,
And strikes the martin with its flame.
I search my memory and say:
Let life be always new again!

The dawn is like a rifleshot
Upon the night. A hissing flame
In air, slow dying in its flight.
Let life be always new again!

The breeze is at the door again,
The same that huddled near our house
At night, and shivered in the rain.
Let life be always new again!

That fellow's singularly odd.
Why does he barge into the guard?
The sign is plain: "No thoroughfare."
Let life be always new again!

Then wave the traffic flag in air,
And play the master for a day,
As long as men this darkness walk,
And while the country is in flames.

1919

It's Spring Out There

It's spring out there, in the street! The poplar stands
Amazed, horizons tremble, houses fear they may fall.
There the air is blue like the bundle of linen
A patient takes home when leaving the hospital.

There the evening's blank, like a story begun
By a star, broken off without a conclusion,
While a thousand riotous eyes stare empty of mind
In immeasurable deep confusion.

1918

Drizzling Rains

The air is whipped by drizzling rains;
The ice, a scabby grey. You gaze
The harder for the sky to waken;
It wakes with wind and storm ablaze.

As always, with overcoat unbuttoned,
With muffler open at the chest,
March drives the screeching birds ahead,
The frenzied birds at every nest.

He's sure to see you, and, untidy,
He'll scrape the candle drippings, squint
And yawn, and say it's safe to take
The cover from your hyacinth.

As always, senseless, in confusion,
He'll ruffle his hair-mop, stammering,
To stun you with scurvy, stupid tales
About me—my coming in the spring.

1918

Poetry

Poetry, I swear an oath to you.
I'll swear until I'm hoarse with pain!
You're not a stiff-shirt, prim sweet singer;
You're summer townsfolk come third-class;
You're suburbs, not a vain refrain.

You're hot like Yamskoi street in May,
Tougher than a soldiers' camp at night,
Where clouds, oppressive, groaning, pass,
Or scamper quickly out of sight.

By curving rails divided, you are
No stale old tune, but suburbs dear
To me where men come home from work
Not gay with song but still with fear.

In the long, long night, even at dawn,
The sprouts of rain get mired in vines,
And scrawl from dripping roofs acrostics,
With bubbles in the rhyming lines.

When undoubted truths, O Poetry,
Are held like buckets at the tap,
The hoarded stream will spout—for me
In my open copybook to trap.

1922

Enigma's Fingernail Mark

Here the trail of enigma's fingernail mark:
"Let me rest for the night; at dawn I'll read
It again, to be clear. Till I wake, no being
Can move the beloved as I when I plead."

You thrilled to the brass of my lips even so,
As an audience is moved by actors in form.
My kiss was like summer, a lingering kiss,
That gradually burst into storm.

I drank like the birds. I sucked till I swooned.
In my gullet the stars, their starry delight.
Thus nightingales, quivering, roll their eyes,
As they drain drop by drop the starry night.

1918

POEMS OF TWO REVOLUTIONS

A Woman Revolutionary
(*prologue*, THE YEAR 1905)

Dull winter days grow shabbier
With late October cold;
The tattered skies hang loose and low
Like curtains worn and old.

So soft the tidings in the snows
On silent eerie ways:
Fair as the air, O Revolution,
The news of wondrous days!

A Jeanne d'Arc from bleak Siberia,
O prisoner in chains,
Who, bold in courage, dared to face
Long exile, grief, and pain!

A socialist, you strike in gloom
From random flints a light.
In fear of dragon fires, your tears
On frozen wastes of night.

Lured by our battle guns and cries
For deliverance and life,
Your message flames the street—your words
Made manifest in strife.

Amidst the festive flags you stand
Alone, elusive, proud.
Like an artist—critic of himself—
You shun the joyful crowd.

The struggle dies. Like a poet, you stride
The night—to win your soul.
You scorn not money-bags alone,
But every trifling role.

1926

Bloody Sunday
(*from* THE YEAR 1905)

Night. Petersburg.
The air swells dark with icy flakes
under needling footsteps;
no street's forbidden
to fur coats or sheepskins plain.
The moon shrinks smaller by half in the frost.
The Neva district stirs.
Crowds clear a way:
He comes! Gapon!

The hall rings loud
in airless heat.
Five thousand in the press.
From the street the blown snow
clings to stairways in the hall.
Here's the new nativity:
against the walls
of a dingy vaulted womb
pulses
a strange unlovely lump—
our newborn age.

A notorious dawn.
Clouds in black and cranberry hues.
Halls and galleries creak,
and slops steam in the streets.
On the run they dash toward the gates
from meeting places
to follow
church banners

in the open cold,
in the blaze
of winter day.

Eight roaring waves
and then the ninth,
majestic as space.
Caps off, they chant as they go,
Save Thy people, O Lord!
Canal and bridge to left;
to right, the graveyard gates;
at rear, soundless trees,
and telegraph wires in front.

Pavements rise on stilts
on Kamennoi Island;
crowds stare from curbs and stalls.
Behind the slow procession
long trails
of crowded streets and lanes.
They near the Palace Park
and march over Trinity Bridge.

Eight volleys from the Neva
and then the ninth,
as weary as glory.
Ho, the cavalry at right and left!
Ho, spaces thunder forth:
Butchers, we'll get even with you!
This is the hour of rending
at the joints
of loyalty sworn
to rulers.

Scurrying sidewalks,
deeper dusk,
and the fallen dead.
On barricades volleys answer
to the cannonade's roar.
I'm fourteen years,
going on fifteen.
Such days are a diary
to be read at will
at any page.

We play a game of snowballs.
We catch flakes spinning
out of the sky—
flakes of hearsay and talk of the times.
We feel this landslide of kingdoms
in the high-school yard,
and the reeling of snows
in January.

Stormwinds day after day.
The lads in the Party
look like eagles
and act grown up.
We, smaller boys,
jeer at our tutors,
push desks to the walls,
play at parliament in class,
and daydream
about forbidden slums of the poor.

For three days running
it snows,
then clears up at night.
Next morning
we hear the shattering news:
Our high-school patron,
Sergei Alexandrich,
shot dead
in the Kremlin. . . .
In those first days in February
I grew up to love the mighty storm.

1925

Mutiny at Sea
(*from* THE YEAR 1905)

In time all matters pall.
But not the sea's immensity.
In the welter of days
and of years and ages,
in the white rage
of waves,
in the white trance
of acacias,
the sea
alone the sea
cuts one down to size.

Your throne, O Sea,
on mounds of nets.
Your shout rings loud in the skies;
you're gay as spring
in play
when breezes wave a fugitive lock
around a sailor's brow
on watch at the prow.
You please the children playful in spray.
Or tossing, you trumpet in storms
when the elements battle
and call you home.

Then the ancient of time
and chaos
in spume of seas,
hoarse with ravenous waves,
dashes with hatred

80

satanic,
a monster roaring with ruin and graves,
and, livid with ooze,
it crumbles the stones at the port.

Sails in their fear of darkness
huddle beneath the walls
of storm and rains.
Skies crouch lower
flying downward
steep
sea slopes
and finger the deep
with wings of clamorous gulls.

Weary the ships come
gasping,
electric with storm and dark
in infernal chaos of clouds;
rocking,
laboring slow,
they heave into port.
Blue-limbed lightnings
leap like toads into pools.
Forerigging and shrouds
shattered—
topsail yard to deck.

Ready for slumber at last.
With evening crabs
stirring for shelter,
and aster heads nodding

in the wearisome sun,
the sea, rippling,
purrs.
The grey-flushed hulk
of a steel-clad battleship
rust-speckled
heaves in the ebb.

Sundown.
The warship *Potémkin*
flamed in sight
electric with light.
From spardeck to mouldy caboose,
invaded by myriads of galley-flies,
tainted stew meat
they served the crew. . . .
Darkness embroiled the sea.
The portholes pitted the darkness;
lights grumbled until daybreak,
then shuddered, and died.

Great mounds of morning surges
glided
like mercurial razors
from the shining hulk.
Towering above them
the battleship waked to the sound of a bell
for morning prayers.
Men shuffled to swab every deck.
At dinner they sulked
in revolt at pots and kettles.
They gulped dry bread and water;

they chewed hardtack in silence.
Then a voice yelled out:
"All hands on deck!
On watch! To your places!"
Someone in white
purple with gall
cursed,
bellowed:
"Attention!

"Not satisfied, eh?
Back to the kettles!
If not, to the yards! Step quick!"
The watch looked dazed.
Sudden, with one impulse, together
they rushed in riot
to the guns.
"Hold back!"
shouted in rage their master and lord.

Some paused in their tracks.
He blocked their escape.
"A plot? Mutiny?"
He yelled a command:
"Ensign! tarpaulin! the haul!
Sentries, the chains!"
Other poor wretches
huddled in the maws of gun towers,
and waited in terror the lash and chains.

Sailor hearts
throbbed in fear.

One lad could stand it no longer,
and in agony shouted:
"Mates! Come on!
Kill them!
To the guns! For liberty!
Fight!"
Men leaped from the turrets
to the decks
for the fight.

And the mutiny winged
like a flame
from mizzen to bridge.
It spurted,
it crackled,
it spanned the air like an arc.
"No backing out!
Look here,
kill the scoundrels!"
Trac-tac-tac! . . .
They picked them off
on the run.

Trac-tac-tac! . . .
Bullets spattered the decks,
or they found their prey
on the waves.
They crackled in air
in broadsides of fire
at their heels,
trac-tac-tac!
Overboard with them!

They jeered:
"Get out to your Navy review!"

Down by the turbines,
hot and eager,
men waited for news,
when, like a stoker's shadow,
towering tall,
Matushénko
peered
into the pits below,
and shouted:
"Okay, Steve! We got 'em!"

Steve clambered up,
and grinning, embraced him.
"We'll do without 'em, don't worry!
A few under guard;
for the rest, the sea.
How's the junior engineer?"
"With us, to be sure."
"Good! Send him to me,
on the bridge."

Day came to a close.
At sunset,
curtained by smoke,
through the tube
a sailor boomed to sailors below:
Anchors! Aweigh!
The voice grew still in the clouds.

The battleship sailed for Odessa,
forging furrows of doom,
rust-speckled,
aglow.

1926

A Testament
(*from* LIEUTENANT SCHMIDT)

"In vain in days of chaos
We look for a happy end:
Some bear their Golgotha;
Some judge, and some repent.

"Like you, I am an atom
In a time of transformation,
And I accept your verdict—
Resigned, without vexation.

"I'm sure you will not falter
To sweep me off your stage,
O martyrs of your dogma,
O victims of your age!

"For thirty years I've cherished
My country's destiny,
Yet I do not ask or hope for
Your magnanimity.

"The days we brood upon,
Remembering their roar,
Were days of surging waves
That hurled me to the fore.

"It was hard to stand aloof,
And harder not to give
My life. I don't regret
The way I chose to live.

"I stand between two eras
At war, and I rejoice:
The post between two camps
I occupy by choice."

1927

Sublime Malady

The moving riddle gleams, and still
The siege goes on, day after day,
For months, with passing of the years.
One winter day the weary pickets
Come shouting, breathless, with the news:
The stronghold has surrendered!
We doubt, believe; estates in flames;
The vaulted rooms are blown to dust.
We search for doors, go in and out,
While days and months and years flit by.
The shadows deepen with the years.
The tale of Troy is born again.
We doubt, believe; estates in flames.
Impatient, some expect the army.
We're weak and blind. Day after day
High prison walls are blown to dust.

I am ashamed, each day ashamed,
That in an age of shadows
Our sublime old malady of thought
Still calls itself a song.
Are alleys, shrill in their upheaval,
Our song of toil and soil—
Our song from books and ages hurled
Against steel bayonets?
But hell is paved with good intentions;
It is our modern view
That if verses too are paved with them
Our sins will be forgiven.

Small talk must wound the ears of silence
Back from the fields of war;
How keen the ears of silence are
The days of desolation know.

In those swift-passing days we had
A lust for rumors. The winter nights
Twitched unweariedly from lice,
As horses twitch their ears.
The ears of silent darkness stirred
For days, ears choked with snow;
We became as fairy tales at night
On restless pillows sweet with mint.

By spring a fear came down upon
Upholstered stalls in concert halls.
Each day turned dingier with slush.
They gurgled, spewed their blood
And muttered secrets in the ears
Of waiting rooms, perhaps of this
And that small chat, of railway fares,
Of soldiers from the front on foot,
The thaw, or anything at all.
One goes to sleep—to wait for death,
But talkers turn up with taller tales.
Galoshes tramp for days in slush.
The lice in mufflers and fur coats
Prick up their ears for news, confound
Half-truth with lies from day to day.

Although the thistle of every dawn
That strove to make its shadows longer

Could scarce by striving hard stretch out
The hours of day; although, as of old,
The boggy road dragged every wheel
Through sands up to the sloping top
Again, to bear it to safer ground
By way of sounder village stakes;
Although the vault of autumn skies
Grew dark, the forests far away,
The evenings cold with damp and haze—
We fooled ourselves!
The easeful slumber of the earth
Was in reality a coma,
A death, a silence of the graves,
Resembling a peculiar stillness
Which shrouds the countryside in sleep
But shudders every now and then
In a vain struggle to remember:
What was it, please, I've tried to say?

Although the ceiling, as before,
In shoring up a chamber-room,
Pulled up the second to the third,
And then the fifth floor to the sixth,
Thus hinting by a show of floors
All's well as ever in the world—
We fooled ourselves!
The climbing waterpipes, I tell you,
Sucked up shrill cries of evil days.
The stench of laurel and soya beans
Cooked in the smoke of newspapers
Defiled for a mile the stale, dull air,

And grumbled: Why, a moment, please,
What did they have to eat today?

And creeping like a hungry tapeworm
From the second floor to the third,
And from the fifth floor to the sixth,
The stench advanced with filth and sloth
To slay the voice of loving-kindness.
What shall we ever do? Our cries
Had vanished in the clanging air,
And, falling on the railway station,
Their tumult passed the water tower
And rows of solitary tombs,
And disappeared beyond the groves
Where the embankments flared like gashes,
Where snowdrifts driven to and fro
Lay piled up high among the pines,
Where iron rails grew blind with itching
By contact with the rising storms.
Behind it all, in a glow of legends,
The wise, the hero, and the fool
Blazoned in print their happiness
About the sunset of their age.

Then knaves and boors began to face
Our past, our ancient past of darkness,
While the snows still busily contended
With death in the murk of endless night.
Like an organ, there upon the ice
Of mirrors the railway station flashed
In secret, staring open-eyed,
Telling about its wretched state

And emptiness, about repairs
And holidays, while striving hard
To keep its looks a little longer.
The intolerable frightful typhus,
Clasping us quietly by the knees,
Mused long and moveless, shuddering,
To hear the running tunes about
The crumbling palaces in dust.
Then from the hollow organ rose,
Like dust within the seams of bellows,
The weary strains of slow decay.
Its faithful and exacting ear
Continued to entreat the mist,
The ice, and pools along the floors,
To keep if possible their silence.

We were that music in the ice:
I speak of my own society
With which I now intend to leave
The stage, as I for one must leave.
There is no room for shame:
I wasn't made to coax three times
And flatter men in sundry ways;
Yet more absurd than any song
Our word "the enemy."
I'm grieved to find in each far land
This malady of mind.
All my life I've longed to be like others,
But the world's great age
Is stronger than my private yearning
And wants to be—like me.

We were the music of the teacups
Come round for tea and cake in shade
Of voiceless trees, in sercet ways
Unworthy of the mind of man.
In winter cold the rooks wheeled high
In stiller skies, but our frosty year,
Ashamed, stood waiting at the gates.
We were the music of ideal thought,
Barren in works; come winter time,
Our indecision turned to ice
The servants' yard and kitchen stairs.

But, hear me! I myself observed
The great Ninth Congress of Soviets.
I ran for hours in slush, I cursed
The streets, I cursed my luck, before
I got there for the second day,
Excited, to see the deputies,
And proud to show my official pass.
In sober mood, by sober roads
I came. Around me lay a city
In ruins, ravaged, and unreal,
Refusing flatly to recover,
To rise, get going, to rebuild.

From posted newspapers on walls
The Karelian problem stared, raising
A question in big-eyed sickly birches.
Like lines of braid, the snow remained
On telegraph poles while winter days
Came slow to their appointed end,
And faded on the forest canvas

In every waiting branch—to set
A good example. At that moment
The moral of the magic canvas
Seemed The Convention in itself,
That the fever of exalted minds
Proves whiter, stronger than cement
If suddenly, after long weeks,
The builders' straining eyes behold
The rising ramparts of a fortress
Or even a trifling little fort.
(Only men who would evade hard labor
May keep their sickly disbelief).

Fresh minds can nourish generations;
But their alluring golden pie,
The while tradition stirs the sauce,
Sticks in our throats and makes us choke.
At last, after a saner view,
We've left behind our witless talk,
The commonplace, our trite set speeches,
Familiar trifles of the day
And disagreements about details.

No longer is the farce prescribed
For me as a self-sufficient cure,
Nor do I now recall the reason
For registering a ready vote.
I have forgotten now the day
When from the deep Pacific, below
The yawning Japanese abyss,
A wire declared the difference
Between workers and the octopi,

(Oh, what an erudite sea-diver!)
Or when those flaming mountain-sides
Seemed not their natural concern.
But many acts are far more foolish
Than trying to classify Pompeii.
I long remember as by rote
That wicked telegram we sent
For victims of the tragedy,—
That hackneyed workers' proclamation
To ease the terror of Fujiyama.

Awake, O Poet! Show your pass!
No dozing, comrade, at this meeting.
Into the pit from boxes rushed
Lovát, Msta, Ládoga, Sheksná.
Through doorways open to the South
Again from the Assembly Hall
The breath of Petrine arctic storms
Convulsed the agitated lamps.
Again the frigate went broadside.
Again, overwhelmed by plunging waves,
The child of treachery and cavil
Accepts no more his native land.

At night, behind the Imperial train,
The hunters and their packs, halloing,
Scattered themselves across the ice
In every region of the coast.
And, hunched, the clink of spurs came on
The scene. Behind the railway bridges,
Behind the railway right of way,
Two-headed eagles hung in veils,

And old traditions hid their fears.
The Pullman cars stood cold in darkness
For hours in desolated fields.
The scent of March was in the air.
At Porkhovo, in wet tarpaulin,
From billows blustering for miles,
A munitions factory awoke
And yawned along the Baltic shore.

In weariness two-headed eagles
Circled above the land of Pskov,
Encompassed, helpless, ringed about
By the great anonymous revolt.
Ah, if they could but find the way
Not given on recorded maps!
But sleepers were in short supply
And dwindled rapidly away;
All they could do was try again
The weakened, crippled railway line.
Spring waters rushed across the tracks.
The future looked too dim and foul.
The circle narrowed; firs grew scarce.
Two suns collided in our windows:
One sun rose over Tosna banks;
A sun went down at Hollow Town.

*   *   *

How shall I end my story now?
I still remember his living voice
That pierced me with encircling flames
Like jagged lightning at the neck.
We rose up with a shout, our eyes

Ransacking thoroughly the platform,
When suddenly he grew—grew taller
Even before he reached the stage.
He entered, unobserved, through lanes
Of crowded doors and helping hands,
As a ball of lightning in a storm
Flames bright and blinding in a room.

The thunder of wild applause rang out
As a relief, like a discharge
Of bursting cannonballs, beyond
Control, uncurled, through rings of space.
He spoke. We honored, we intoned
The memory of our heroic dead.
All that in passing. What force, I ask,
Bound every man to him alone?

His words came like a rapier's thrust.
And, pressing home a point, he struck
Out hard, his thumb hooked in his vest;
His foot swung slowly up and down.
His words could have been about crude oil,
And yet his arching frame was winged
With essential truth, his homely talk
Tearing at the husks of falsehoods
And man's obtuse illusion. His burr,
His words, which all men heard too well,
Were traced in the blood of great events.
He was their voice, their proclamation.
In envy only of the ages,
And jealous of their jealousy

Alone, he ruled the tides of thought,
And through that mastery—the State.

What secret threads unite as one
Past ages and the present years!
Great men are heralds of new rights—
And burdens too as they leave the stage.

1923-28

ABOVE THE BARRIERS

Poems of Various Years

The Drowsy Garden

The drowsy garden scatters beetles
Bronze as the ashes from a pan.
Level with me and with my candle
Hang flowering universes. Then,

As into some unheard-of faith
I pass the threshold of that night,
Where grizzled with decay, the poplar
Screens away the edges of moonlight,

Where lies the pond—an open secret,
Where billows of the apple sigh,
Where as a house on piles the garden
Holds up the mansion of the sky.

1914

Winter Skies

In a week, the starry river is one
Hard sheet of ice in dim blue light.
The skaters, tumbling, sprawl; the fields
Clink glasses with the sounding night.

Go easy, easy, eas-i-er, skaters,
Who cut your daring figures, and try
With grinding skates to grave at turnings
A constellation in a Norway sky.

The air and night seem chained with steel
Together. Beware, O skaters! You know
The night spreads far a copra's orbit
Around the earth, like a bone domino.

With howling of a dog frost-bitten,
The moon will freeze on iron heels,
And stuffed like liars' jaws with lava
Of breathless ice, each mouth congeals.

The Soul

As I now recall it, a jailbird set free;
And lest I forget it, a captive of time.
A spirit, a pilgrim, as many believe;
But for me, a shade from a homelier clime.

I may try to bury you under a stone
Of verses, in dust! But prisoned, you dwell
Sublime in your struggle, a true Tarakánova
When the river in springtime flooded her cell.

O Prisoner, pleading for pardon in gloom
And charging the times and guards at the bar!
While vanishing years fall away like leaves
By the garden hedge of our calendar.

Snow Storm

In this suburb here where no foot dares go,
Where wizards rave and the snow storm blows,
Here in this circle of fury and frenzy
Where slumber deep snows, like the slain in rows;

In this suburb here that you know, where no foot
Dares go, where only the wizards and storms
Blow wild, a leathern thong at the window
Flaps like a wanderer crazed by the storm.

No light in the streets and yet this suburb
May be in the city, in Moscow, or near
The bridge in the outskirts. (My guest who came
At midnight recoils from me in his fear.)

But, mark, in the suburb here where no foot
Dares go, where only murderers meet,
A leaf of the aspen—the voiceless leaf
Is thy herald, a phantom more pale than a sheet!

It tumbles about in the whirlwind of streets
And batters on gateways, longing for light.—
Not this the city, the city remembered,
O herald, forerunner, lost in the night!

Not in vain, O herald, thy message to me
In this suburb where now no man dares go,
Where I too am lost—so alien the night
And the City remembered of storm and snow.

1915

The Urals for the First Time

In darkness, no midwife to help, pressing
Its hands against gloom, the Ural fastness
Half-dead with agony was screaming
In blindest pain at the birth of morning.

Tall ranges, loosed by chance, and the bronze
Of massive shadows came rumbling down.
A panting locomotive; the spectral fir trees
Swerved, stumbling, hurled by piercing shrieks.

An opiate the smoky dawn—no less,
Plied by a huge flame-breathing dragon
To factories and mountain summits—
Like a traveler doped by a practiced thief.

The flames of sunrise. From poppy-red skies
Like hunters on skis, they licked the foothills;
They suddenly lighted the firs with crowns,
And roused them to enter their kingdom again.

In glory arrayed, the shaggy dynasts
Of firs stood rank by rank, and trod
The orange velvet of carpeted snows
And tinseled cloth and damask.

1915

Spring Days

How many small buds like candle-butts
Fast glued to the boughs around!
Warm April days. The park has the savor
Of puberty, blaring with sound.

The forest is roped, in a noose of shrill
Small throats, as a lassoed buffalo,
And groans in the nets like a steely wrestler
In an organ throbbing sonatas slow.

Oh, poetry, be in my life like a sponge
With a suction pad that cleaves,
Drinks in, on a wet green bench in the garden
Alone with gummy young leaves.

Swell splendid with ruffles, lawns, clouds,
With trilling valleys converse.
At night I will squeeze your substance out
On thirsty white paper in verse.

Three Movements

1

When you probe each day for trifles,
Detail by detail, to the lees,
Then the sultry chatter of squirrels
Rings shrill in the resinous trees.

And languid, waxing in strength,
The pine trees drowse in a row,
While the forest boughs are peeling,
And their freckled sweat drips slow.

2

The garden's sick with miles of torpor.
The palsied hollows in their rages
Are fiercer far than hurricanes,
Than savage raids the tempest wages.

The storm draws near. The shriveled mouths
Of gardens taste dry nettles, fear,
Decay, and thatch. The cattle's bellow
Mounts in pillars of burning air.

3

Now the driven clouds in tatters
Grow on bushes in the groves.
Damp nettles fill the garden's mouth—
Smell of rain and treasure-troves.

No more wailing in the copses;
Now the air is clear on high.

Like a wading bird the blue
Barefoot walks across the sky.

And the oak and willow glisten,
And the bush is blossoming!
Like glistening moist lips,
Like tracks beside the spring.

Improvisation

I fed out of my hand a flock of keys
To clapping of wings and shrill cries in flight.
Sleeves up, arms out, on tiptoe I rose;
At my elbow I felt the nudging of night.

The dark. And the pond, and the wash of waves.
And screeching black beaks in their savage attack,
All quick for the kill—not to hunger and die,
While birds of the species I-love-you fall back.

The pond. And the dark. The pulsating flare
From pipkins of pitch in the gloom of midnight.
The boat's keel nibbled by lapping of waves.
And birds at my elbow in their wrath and fight.

Night gurgled, washed in the gullets of weirs.
And it seemed if the young were unfed, by rote,
The hen-birds would kill—before the roulades
Would die in the shrilling, the crooked throat.

1915

To a Friend

Come, don't I know that, stumbling in the shadows,
Our night will never change again to light?
Am I a monster? And is the good of millions
Less dear to me than anyone's selfish right?

And don't I make the Five-Year Plan my plan
And goal, sink with its fall, rise with its rise?
But what about myself? Shall I be free?
Be worse than our inertia, content likewise?

In vain in these days of the Supreme Soviet
Where thought and passion have a place of pride,
You leave a seat in honor of the poet:
That place is dangerous—if not unoccupied!

1931

To Anna Akhmátova

It seems I'm choosing the essential words
That I can liken to your pristine power.
And if I err, it's all the same to me,
For I shall cling to all my errors still.

I hear the constant patter on wet roofs,
The smothered eclogue of the wooden pavements.
A certain city comes clear in every line,
And springs to life in every syllable.

The roads are blocked, despite the tide of spring
All round. Your clients are a stingy, cruel lot.
Bent over piles of work, the sunset burns;
Eyes blear and moist from sewing by a lamp.

You long for the boundless space of Ládoga,
And hasten, weary, to the lake for change
And rest. It's little in the end you gain.
The canals smell rank like musty closet-chests.

And like an empty nut the hot wind frets
Across their waves, across the blinking eyelids
Of stars and branches, posts and lamps, and one
Lone seamstress gazing far above the bridge.

I know that eyes and objects vary greatly
In singleness and sharpness, yet the essence
Of greatest strength, dissolving fear, is the sky
At night beneath the gaze of polar light.

That's how I call to mind your face and glance.
No, not the image of that pillar of salt
Exalts me now, in which five years ago
You set in rhymes our fear of looking back.

But as it springs in all your early work,
Where crumbs of unremitting prose grew strong,
In all affairs, like wires conducting sparks,
Your work throbs high with our remembered past.

1928

To M. T.

You're right to turn your pockets out
And say: "Well, rummage, feel, and search."
All's one to me why mists are damp.
Any tale would do—a day in March.

The trees in their soft overcoats
Stand planted in gamboge, secure,
Although the branches find for certain
The burden's painful to endure.

The branches shiver with the dews
Rippling like fleece upon merinos;
The dews run shuddering like hedgehogs
Bearing dry haycocks on their noses.

All's one to me whose talk and chatter
The winds from nowhere, blowing, bring,
What rumors muffled now in mists
I hear in every backyard spring.

All's one to me what kind of suits
The fashion holds to be the style.
The hearsays boxing in the poet
Like dreams will vanish in a while.

While rolling on through many channels,
By every fateful turn and bend
He'll drift like smoke from pit to pit
To another threatening dead end.

Like steam he'll rise through fateful clefts
On top, though flattened in the heat,
And in the future men will say:
"His age was burning up like peat."

1928

Balzac

Paris exults in riches, business;
The rains, like vengeance, lull the air.
The pollen flies through sallow streets.
And wrathful bloom the chestnut trees.

The heat as with a glaze incrusts
The horses and the cracking whips;
Like peas piled in a sieve, the heat
Quivers in windows deep embrasured.

Tilburies rush in headlong flight.
Sufficient unto the day the hates:
Why fret about tomorrow's sunrise?
There wrathful bloom the nightmare trees.

But he, their debtor and their hostage,
Where is he hiding?—That alchemist!
As over books, his hulking figure
Curves over dusky alley slums.

He stretches like a poplar, puzzled,
As though to scan the ten commandments;
He spins for Paris, like a spider,
A rich commemorative mass.

He stares below, in agitation,
Spindle-shaped his wakeful eyes.
He spins like hempen fiber threads
The stories of Parisian haunts.

Should he negotiate his ransom
From the yoke of dreaded creditors,
He'll fade to nothingness and lose
His scope and meaning thread by thread.

What made him truly take on credit
Parisian crowds, the Stock Exchange,
The fields, the village unconstraint
At feasts among the willow trees?

He dreams of freedom like a valet,
Like an old clerk who counts his pension—
This man of massive mind, this man
Whose hands hang heavy as a mason's.

When will he wipe his sweat away,
Renounce the rot of coffee-houses,
And, fending off all care and thought,
Follow Saint Matthew chapter six?

1927

Sailing Away

We hear the lisping salt-sea drip.
Still mute and low the throbbing wheel.
Gently we take the harbor's shoulders
Past warehouses and twilight hill.

The swish and splash of tideless waters.
The birch bark's sailing onward. Higher
The rollers, moaning, rush behind us,
Foaming pale-rose, on fire.

The crunch and crack of crayfish shells;
The birchen hiss in sunset glow.
The great sea mounts; bending, it shudders
With swelling tides below.

The shores recede in scrubby pines
And wretched groves to right and left.
In gloomy sluggishness sea waves,
Indifferent, regard our craft.

A billowing long roller strikes
The starboard dumb, and passes on—
To glide along the wooded beaches,
To gather cloudberries in the sun.

About us still the shore line swims
To mark our voyage, and never strange
The shores we know. But not for long.
Our course grows menacing with change.

We take a dread half circle to
New tides and far-off boundaries:
The masts ride out between the gates
Of surging, racing open seas.

At last, the sea! And like an omen
Of storms and changes, suddenly
Above the grievous chasms, a gull
Drops like a stone, and scoops the sea.

The Gulf of Finland
1922

O Great Marksman

O great marksman, O vigilant hunter,
Phantom with a gun on the spirit's flood!
Spare me—one in a hundred—spare from
Crushing my life in your lust for blood.

Let me surmount a shameful death.
Hide me in willow and ice at night.
Start me at dawn from a lakeside brake.
Kill on the wing! But kill outright!

My thanks to you, O peoples disdained,
At our parting in my splendid flight!
I embrace in shyness friend and neighbor,
My country and kin in the hour of night.

1928

Cocks

All night the water labored without a stop.
Till dawn the rain has burned its linseed oil.
In waves of lilac steam, the earth smokes like
A pot of cabbage soup that's near the boil.

But when the grasses, trembling, leap up again,
Who will my terror to the dew attest
As the first cock begins to crow, and then
Another, a third, and after him the rest?

And when the cocks from out the darkness call
Each in his turn, and probe each year by name,
Their crowing augurs clear the change to come—
To rain, to earth, to love, to each and all.

1923

Lilies of the Valley

Since dawn the day's grown hot. You part
The bushes, and the heavy noon
Will crack its leaden weight behind you,
And splinter from the diamond strokes.

It topples, edge-long, glittering,
In dappled spots of trembling light,
Like a heavy box of glass let fall
From sweaty shoulders to the ground.

White bodies canopied at night
Beneath these eaves appear coal black.
But spring's a fairyland of new
Incomparable loveliness.

The savage carnage of the heat
Stops at the edges of the grove.
You gaze at every birch you meet,
And they attentively gaze back.

But you have been forestalled. Someone
Is watching shyly near the ground:
A ravine lies studded by a shower
Of dew-wet lilies of the valley.

It lies, apart, with its suspended
Clusters of bells—a finger wide,
Or wide as two above the leaves,
One and a half above the roots.

The lilies ripple soundlessly,
Like kidskin, tender as brocade;
The shadows of the twilight grove
Receive them as their evening gloves.

1927

Lyubka

The rain came lately through this forest clearing
Like a surveyor's party. With tinsel threads
It weights the lily of the valley's leaves,
And water's in the mullein's furry ears.

These nurselings of the frosty firs pull down
Their ear lobes with the early evening dews;
They shun the day, prefer to grow apart,
And even waft their fragrance one by one.

And when at evening tea, in summer homes,
The mosquito's sails fill out with mist, and night,
Plucking the strings of a guitar by chance,
In milky darkness stands among the pansies,

The world grows sweet with evening violets:
The years and faces come to mind. And thoughts.
Each thing that may be rescued from the past,
And in the future granted us by Fate.

1927

SECOND BIRTH

WAVES:

1. Here All Things Meet

Here all things meet: The past I have
So long endured, the truths I now
Live by, my values, aspirations,
The whole of life that I avow.

I greet the sea. The infinite.
The boundless sea in light, in gloom.
The mournful cadence. The surges bake
New waves like waffles of the foam.

They rove like sheep along the shore
In endless flocks, forced by the still
Deep sky. He drove them out to pasture
And stretched himself along the hill.

In droves, rolled as in curving tubes,
My truths and deeds return to me
Along the runways of my anguish,
The crests of my grief and agony.

The waves run boundless, endless, charged
With change sublime, their destiny
In time unknown, but in their song
I hear the far-resounding sea.

2. I Would Go Home Again

I would go home again—to rooms
With sadness large at eventide,
Go in, take off my overcoat,
And in the light of streets outside

Take cheer. I'll pass the thin partitions
Right through; yes, like a beam I'll pass,
As image blends into an image,
As one mass splits another mass.

Let all abiding mooted problems
Deep rooted in our fortunes seem
To some a sedentary habit;
But still at home I brood and dream.

Again the trees and houses breathe
Their old refrain and fragrant air.
Again to right and left old winter
Sets up her household everywhere.

Again by dinner time the dark
Comes suddenly—to blind, to scare,
To teach the narrow lanes and alleys
She'll fool them if they don't take care.

Again, though weak my heart, O Moscow,
I listen, and in words compose
The way you smoke, the way you rise,
The way your great construction goes.

And so I take you as my harness
For the sake of raging days to be,
That you may know our past by heart
And like a poem remember me.

3. We Came To Georgia

We came to Georgia. You'll know this land
If hell you multiply by paradise,
Real want by tenderness, and turn a hothouse
Into a base supporting peaks of ice.

And then you'll understand what subtle doses
We ask of duty, work, success—and air,
United properly with earth and sky,
For man to be the way we find him here;

That he may rule himself even in bondage,
In famine and defeat without a fault,
And thus become a model in the ages—
A man in sturdiness as plain as salt.

4. The Caucasus

The Caucasus lay vast in light.
It seemed a rumpled bed, the glow
Of azure ice more fathomless
Than chasms of stagnant heat below.

In mists and out of sorts, it reared
The hatreds of its icy crests
In steady automatic action,
Like salvos from machine-gun nests.

And gazing at this beauty, seeing
Brigades of labor in a race
To win new triumphs, how I envied
The obstacles they had to face.

Oh, if we had their sort of luck!
If, out of time, this age of ours,
This plan, might scrutinize our labor,
As this gigantic mountain lowers!

Then day and night before my vision
Our plan would march, its heel upon
The substance of my prophecies,
Shaping my life and my renown.

There'd be no time for us to wrangle,
To face suspicion, or to forgive;
Instead of merely writing verses,
I would my poems truly live.

5. Socialism

Here—now—our age of socialism!
Here in the thick of life below.
Today in the name of things to be
Into the future forth we go.

Like Georgia shining in her beauty,
Like a land of light by open seas,
It beckons—veiled within a mist
Of wild surmise and theories.

There mothers of Putivl no more
Lament like cuckoos their dismay;
There joy no longer looks askance
In fear, but walks abroad by day.

There life and happiness converse
Together, free from hate and strife,
All joined to give their saving strength
And stay to every child and wife.

There men no longer by exchange
Compute the things they have or owe,
But gladly spend themselves in giving—
The all they have, the all they know.

Then let my message overtake
This wondrous age in history:
O may my children in their gladness
Out of the future answer me!

6. Things of Great Worth

Things of great worth shall come to pass
By true foreknowledge and in fact,—
Names worthier than mine in fame
And words which earned me men's esteem.

Here breakers roar across the bay;
Wave follows wave unchangeably,
Their tracks, like letters traced in sand,
Erased by ebbing lines of foam.

So yet you're here at this resort.
I should have found you in this hall
At five, instead of vain small talk
I shared and wagging of my tongue.

I would have warned you, one so fair,
Mature, a woman brave and calm,
About the death in life—and bounds
No higher than the ant's low life.

Great poets, through experience,
Find words so simple and restrained
That in the end they can't do more
Than wait in silence and in awe.

In faith and kinship with real life
And with the future knit as one,
We're bound to find immortal words
Of unbelievable simplicity.

Yet keep them holy in your hearts
Or we shall not be spared at all.
Men quickly grasp the complex schemes
When simplicity's their greater need.

1932

The Death of a Poet

They mumbled, doubted, said he raved.
They did not judge him from another,
No, not at all. They equated him
And his premeditated end
With bureaucrats, shop-women, flats,
With lodgings, lanes, with crows in trees
That rage in reeking noonday heat
In anger at fool intruding crows
To stop their chatter, mind their own,
To leave what happened alone, alone.
A show of tepid grief their looks,
Like creases formed in broken dreams.

So calm, so fair the face of day,
That fairest day, your day of death!
They shuffled, crowded, lined the stairs;
Your gunshot lined them in the halls.

Asleep, your bed their common gossip.
Asleep, from agony unloosened, calm,
O handsome, O twenty-two-year-old
Foretold in your own tetraptych long!

You lay asleep, face to the wall,
Asleep, who, poised, at one great bound,
Flashed, charging, first among the ranks,
With youth in splendid fame aligned.
Your leap was plain, was manifest,
Your glory in your leap revealed.
Your shot, like Aetna, burst upon
Foothills of cringing, frightened fools.

1930

Don't Worry About Me

Don't worry about me, don't weep,
Do not torture your withering heart.
You live in my spirit as a friend,
As my solace, and never apart.

For my faith in the future is real,
Plain-spoken and free. Let us act,
Not saving our pride and illusions,
But honoring life in fact.

Away with your typhoid mattress!
Be a friend to the sun! Acclaim
As a brother the air, all your own
As a letter addressed in your name.

Tear it open, then, like a letter;
Correspond with horizons of air
In the language of Alpine spaces,
And conquer your pain and despair.

In your feast of skies and of lakes,
In the marrow of mountain peaks,
You will learn I'm not a scribbler
Of words in the manner of freaks.

Good luck to you, dear! In your world,
Like a shoot growing straighter each day
In the sun—not under my roof—
You will judge in a different way.

Dear Love's a Heavy Cross

Dear love's a heavy cross at times,
But you are lovely, plain and free;
As true as any key to life,
The secret of your grace to me.

Spring comes with rustling in the night,
With living truth and tidings fair.
From such a fountain-head your race;
Your mind's impartial as the air.

To wake at ease, to find new sight,
Shake off the scum of idle chatter,
And live unspotted in the world—
No need for craft in such a matter.

1931

And Still It Snows!

And still it snows! Endure, and grin!
No matter, storm or rain in floods,
I'll make my darling's modest table
Rich with bitter poplar buds.

Let darkness drip its liquor now,
The soup, with cut-up fennel sour,
The glasses dizzy with our clatter
And babble of the sweeping shower.

We should have punched the crazy snow,
And, deafened by our noise and play,
Unstopped the mouldy window frames
Like bottled wine, and hailed the day.

Bring in the noisy street! And damn
The weather! Take your ease from toil
And trouble now! Let sunlight flood
The salad dish with asphalt oil.

Then, behind Ilya's bumping chariot
Light-rumbling in the sky, I guess
My calflike ecstasies will gallop
Beside your calflike tenderness.

1931

Darkness of Death

The darkness of death.
By the side of curbings
In ditches—the bodies
Of sunken roofs.

Sashes of cabins,
And the ochre of rooms
In a morgue of pools
As wide as streams.

There cabbies lie
And their painted carts,
And the fiery horses
Of faraway skies.

And raindrops on bushes
And a street in clouds,
The chirrup of birds
And buds on branches.

They come together,
Together with me,
Down desolate highways
To Yamskoi field.

Where lampposts drowse,
Where the azure's alien,
The bullfinches deafen
The air at dawn.

Once more the land
In meekness, in silence,
In her mighty labor
Offers her gifts.

1931

Gay Shawls and Shoes

Gay shawls and shoes, the burning gaze
Of snowdrops round—they stir my blood!
Not flat with the water level runs
The rusty chocolate of mud.

The slush in sunlight kneads our spring
And the drowsy noise of stones, while sands
And streams will knead the call of birds
As cooks shape dumplings in deft hands.

Gay shawls and flounces—all in plenty!
The thawing earth's black liquorice.
I praise Thy name a hundredfold,
And, like a stream, break free of ice.

And when I'm high above the level,
I'll thank Thee till I'm hoarse, yet deign
To sink Thy world as in a mirror,
Reflected in my thanks again.

Put an end to curbs, an end to gutters
In spit and froth, an end to crowds,
To the crescent azure of the skies,
To empty shadows of the clouds,

To the gelatine of blind noon hours,
To yellow glass of pools, to lines
Of slender mica of the icefields,
And to hillocks girt by dusky vines.

1931

The Fumes of Vain Renown

O love, the fumes of vain renown
Are to me as pits of reeking flame.
But you are like a dictionary,
My source of secret, hidden fame.

But oh for stronger growth, deep down
Among the roots! . . . All talk apart,
In kinship true, I have my fame
And partnership in home-bred art.

Contemporaries not of poets,
The byways, lanes, and hedges rhyme
Our Pushkin now with snows and geese,
And Lermontov with summer time.

I wish the more that after death
When from this life we draw apart,
They may rhyme together you and me
Closer than auricle and heart.

May our tale of love that alters not
Proclaim our names, and never pass—
How as one we sucked the sap of life,
And will suck in aftertime the grass.

1931

O Love, My Best

O Love, my Best, so real to me,
So dear your beauty, and so fair!
It craves the favor of a rare
Sweet rhyme and lines of melody.

We live, we fade away like rhymes,
But truth in life for you and me
Abides, despite our jarring times.

A rhyme's no echo in a line.
'Tis but a rightful token sign
To occupy a place of worth
With roots in our immortal earth.

And do you doubt my rhyme to love
And all-enduring life is due?
Let stormy brows and eyes reprove
Or mournfully bewail and rue!

A rhyme's no chiming echo for
A line; a rhyme's an open door,
A hallway where you leave behind
Your wraps, your trifles of the mind,
Your heavy burdens, pain, and shame,
And rumors trumpeting your name.

O Love, my Best, so dear you are,
So real your beauty is to me,
You draw my song on wings afar—
My happy song of ecstasy.

Polyclitus long enshrined your praise,
Your sovereign grace from sea to sea.
Your sovereign grace of ancient days
I've known through all Eternity.

1931

There Is No One in That House

There is no one in that house,
Only twilight. Only one:
Winter's in the drafty rooms
Where the curtains are undrawn.

Only grey cold damp is sweeping
In the emptiness below.
Only roofs, the snow; nothing
Besides the roofs and snow.

And the hoarfrost in the night
Comes with storms of winter near.
Conflicts of the long ago,
And the sadness of last year,

Sting my contrite heart with wrongs
And with unforgiven blame. . . .
Still my want of wood for burning
Will not spare the window frame.

Then the curtained door will shudder
Sudden with impending doom.
You will enter like the future,
Pace the silence of the room.

You will come inside my doorway,
Dear in something white, and plain;
Truly like a flake of snow,
Come in something white again.

1931

You're Here at Last

You're here at last, a presence near
To me, to breathe the selfsame air
Again; near as our Kiev outside
The window, wrapped in sultry light;

As Kiev, restless in its sleep,
Striving, unconquered, by its will
To make the sweaty silken collar
Fall brick by brick from off its neck;

As Kiev, sweating in its leaves,
And free at last, with poplar trees
Along victorious avenues
Foregathered, weary, in a crowd.

Your mind and mien are like our Dnieper
Green-belted by its trails and groves;
You are my book of deep-down roots
And faithful entries day by day.

Today your presence is my call
At once to sit down by your side,
And, reading slowly from A to Z,
To write your presence in my book.

1931

146

Vision of Tiflis

Twilight. The mettlesome hazels
In profusion spread. We beheld
In wonder a magic vista
And paused to gaze at the scene.

On precipitous falls, as ever,
Young woods were wantonly climbing
In sport uphill to the summit,
Trampling the rotting stumps.

The telegraph limped, crippled
As ever in its porcelain nests;
Air drifted, scrambling and panting
And tossing its wych-elm's braids.

Under shattered shadows of hazel
There, as ever, in looping array
The reddening highway wheeled onward
And twisted in evening dusk.

Every rise and fall warned of danger;
Every boulder, a lurking thief.
The buffalo, straining full tilt,
Sailed past like a naked devil.

In the sky, like serpents on eggs,
Clouds coiled in rings, more dread
Than the ranges of dragon shadows,
Than the forage of ancient Tartars.

The ranges were gravestones risen
On a background of snow-bound trails
Beyond the ethereal regions
Where Prometheus languished in death.

Like souls of the dead arisen
In ranks the glaciers appeared,
And the sun in India ink
Recorded the ghosts in its book.

Then we four on the hanging steep
Turned as one to gaze in the depths;
Like black spots on a blade, below
Tiflis gleamed dark in a chasm.

It flouted the upper realms,
It mocked all creation, seeming
Like a tapered chimera below,
A city of a world unknown;

As though, surviving by tribute,
Its soul turned cold through the ages
When Tamerlane over the mountains
Led his hosts to battle of old;

As if evening laid bare on a plain
Its fortunes under Persian fire;
The roofs gleamed raspberry red,
And it swarmed as an ancient host.

1931

Had I Known It Once for All

Oh, had I known it once for all
Before my career began, how chill
With death the lines of passion, how
They grip you at the throat and kill,

I would have pointedly refused
To mask by craft my secret aim.
We hesitate in doubt at first,
And dread the lure of early fame.

But this grey age, like Rome, instead
Of jests and twaddle and the lie
Mouthed in stagey lines, demands
The actor must in earnest die.

When passion is the play, it brings
To walk the stage a man unfree;
And then the lines are not of art,
But earth and life and destiny.

1931

When I Grow Weary

When I grow weary of their empty chatter
And turncoat common flattery, I long
For life again—my tender sunlight dreams,
For memories of things once real in life.

In ways unknown, and by its will alone,
I had the sense of exalted enterprise:
Not by my private choice or special gift
I made the larger good my own true faith.

Then came the time of our constructive plans;
Winter again, the fourth year in its turn.
Two women, seared, in light of table lamps,
Like ghost-fires with their burdens gleam and burn.

We live in days to come, I tell them firmly,
And share one lot in common now. If crippled,
No matter! Stay. We are in fact run over
By the New Man in the wagon of his Plan.

And if from death no medicine will save us,
Then time, uncurbed, will rush more free into
The far unknown where the second Five-Year Plan
May long defer the thesis of man's soul.

Then do not mourn in vain! No, do not grieve!
Despite my helplessness, I live in you.
We shall outlive, in the face of all misfortune,
The last of plagues that brought us down.

1932

Hurry, My Verses, Hurry!

Hurry, my verses, hurry! Never
Have I so needed you before.
For there's a house where days are torn
Asunder in the heart's deep core,
Where work is ended, where they wait
And weep in helplessness their fate.

A bitter bromide there they drink
Like water, sleepless, and they sink.
You know—the house of bitter fare!
You know—be quick, and hurry there!

Let storms of winter whoop and stun,
Only hurry like a rainbow; run
Like a dream, a bit of cheerful news;
Because I love her—don't refuse!

Our women bear great miseries,
Saddled by ancient fetishes!
I know the crushing living pain
Of evil galling them to death!
Yet all my life I've choked my wrath
Against their meekness and their chains.
I say they are fooled by common lying
And tales of nature slow in dying,
That Bluebeard's real and stronger far
Than all my printed verses are.

And yet, unreal as Gogol's *Viy*,
It's still our frightful heritage,
A phantom of the loathsome past,
Enduring in our fantasy
As woman's fate from age to age,
Believed in fact among the best.

How brave she was, my love how fair!
And though beneath her mother's wing,
She gave her trust and childish glee,
Her days of peace unfearingly,
And, yes, her love! How fancy-free
She gave in play, unreasoning,
Her little world of trust and care!

1931

152

EARLY TRAINS

and

THE VAST EARTH

The Poet's Stubborn Temper

I like the poet's stubborn temper
When he's by nature true and strong:
He feels ashamed to deal in phrases,
Ashamed of his books of hollow song.

And every one will know his face.
He cannot play at hide and seek,
Retreat, withdraw into the past,
Hide in a cellar like a sneak.

He cannot bury his destiny.
Uncertain at the start, his fame,
Increasing slowly with the years,
In his lifetime wins a laureled name.

Then who is he? His trials in what
Arena, for what cause unknown?
And why his striving, why? with whom?—
With himself, within his soul alone.

Like a shore by the Gulfstream warmed,
He is compact of earth and heat.
Time swept the sea into his bay—
Great tides of matter in a heap.

He yearns for freedom, days of peace.
But all his trials come in troops
Like clouds above his workshop table,
Where, hunched against the day, he stoops.

1936

Ages. He Appears

Ages. He appears. *Ghelaty*.
Torches blaze, advance, retreat.
Who led hosts of warring peoples
Forth before his judgment seat?

Other ages. Generations.
Later peoples in a stream.
In their sluggish ears he whispers
Tender phrases of his dream:

"I am not a story-maker,
Nor with trifling warnings come.
Time will spare my style of writing
From your carping curry-comb.

"Are the gates of epochs closed,
Temples shuttered as before?
Yet my steed will reach your porches,
Reined in flight beside your door.

"I am not a ballad-babbler,
Not a strummer at your gate.
I will watch your ranks in battle
From a summit dark with fate.

"At a touch upon the bridle
Far my steed will bear me flying;
I will brave your desert spaces
Still in timeless darkness lying."

Like a thunderstorm enfolding
Death and passion, life and mission,
He will compass lands and spirits,
And deathless live in men's tradition.

His advance, transforming nature,
Neath his hoofs of ringing steel
Will awaken speechless places
And exalt each commonweal.

Cities, byways, huts and houses,
Every zone and market-place,
Every poplar, every doorway,
Soon will know him face to face.

How Good to Be of a Piece
(*from* SUMMER NOTES)

How good to be of a piece,
Never a mere outsider,
To feel from childhood days
Blood kinship with the poor.

I've missed it all, and yet
I never did worm my way
To swagger in their ranks
Or sup with common folk.

A people shaped my soul
And bound me with a hymn,
Not asking if our ties
In love and faith would hold.

A people's like a house
Unfenced; we seldom mark
How small our tent in space,
How infinite the blue.

A people's like a forest
Where we as children find
A name and habitation
For happenings and things.

We're nothing—one by one.
A people hammers out
And fashions for its ends
Our secret aims and dreams.

1936

158

Summer Day

In springtime we prepare small fires
For gardens in the making,
With prayers for a summer harvest
The pagan altars waking.

In steam the virgin furrows glisten,
Prepared since early morning;
The earth's red-hot from end to end
Like a kitchen oven burning.

I throw my shirt aside—to work
Wherever labor takes me;
The heat bears down upon my back
And like wet clay it bakes me.

I stand with sunrays in my eyes
Beneath the noontide blazing;
From head to foot I'm like a pot
The potter's hand is glazing.

When dusk comes, darkling, in my room,
Within my sleeping quarters,
It fills me brimful like a pitcher
With lilac and with water.

Night wipes away the coat of heat
From cooling walls in shade,
And brings me forth, an offering
For any country maid.

1941

The Pines

In grass, amid the balsam pines,
Asters, and burdock heads, we lie
With arms flung back, in quiet rest,
Our faces to the open sky.

Along the pinetree glades, the grass
Grows dense between the tangled roots.
Our eyes meet casually; we change
Our places and our attitudes.

Thus, for a time immortal here,
We receive the sacrament of pines,
Made free from all assaults of plagues
And death within the greenwood shrines.

Like sweet ointment, the azure sky
With studied regularity
Comes down in dappled silver light
And gaily blotches you and me.

We share the peace of pinetree glades,
The ants' unresting thoroughfare,
The drowsy fragrant spice of pines
And laudanum and lemon air.

So frenzied are the flaming tongues
Of sunrays in the pines, we lie
Unmoving, silent, arms flung back,
Our faces to the open sky.

So vast the world before our eyes,
Far spaces and tranquility,
That somewhere past the pinewood trees
And glades I dream a far-off sea.

The waves rise higher than the trees,
And, tumbling from a squally steep,
They hurl their waterspouts and crayfish
From whirlpools of the troubled deep.

At eve, on sunset trails, in tow
The cavalcades of sunrays ramble;
They shimmer in bright codfish oil
And darkling hues of cloudy amber.

In gathered dusk the moon inters
Each trace of daytime revery
Beneath white magic points of foam
And darker magic of the sea.

The waves surge high in fiercer gales,
But round a posted circular
The throngs are crowded on a raft,—
Its scope unmeaning from afar.

1941

False Alarm

Rattling tubs and buckets,
Fuss at early hours.
Dreary evening dampness
After sundown showers.

Stifled tears and sorrow
Crushing day by day.
Whistling locomotives
Many miles away.

Twilight ranges over
Garden trees, and yards
Messy with old scraps
And late autumn shards.

Through the daytime hours
Cries of dull despair
Near the churchyard graves
Pierce the autumn air.

When a widow's wailing
Drifts across the heath,
All my blood cries out
In the face of death.

From my window seat,
Watching year by year,
Through her grief I vision
That my end draws near.

Stormy ways lie open
Where lone winter grieves,
Bitter in the yellow
Dread of driven leaves.

1941

Early Winter Days

The door came open and the kitchen
Was filled with waves of frosty cold,
And, as in childhood on such evenings,
The world quite suddenly grew old.

Dry days and stillness. In the street
About five steps away, grey Winter
Stands timid in uncertainty
As one who doesn't dare to enter.

It snows, and all is new again.
Like blind old men without a guide
Or staff, the willows seem to wander
Into November space outside.

The stream's now ice; the osier freezes.
Above the naked ice looms high
The darkened overarching mirror
Of the infinite and vaulted sky.

But under it a birch tree leans
Beside the road; in loneliness,
With bright stars fastened in her hair
She gazes in that looking glass.

She long surmises, as her secret,
He brings surprises on the sly
To cottage folk, as wonderful
As are his wonders in the sky.

1941

164

Hoarfrost

Dull days in a flutter of leaves.
The last geese in wedges take wing.
It's foolish to worry: old fears
Have the roundest big eyes in the world.

Let the wind that cradles the rowan
Still frighten its nurseling at night.
The surface of nature's delusive,
Like a tale with a happy conclusion.

Tomorrow you'll wake up at dawn,
And, watching the vastness of snow,
You'll stand again by the well,
In amazement, rooted to earth.

A season of swarming white flakes,
White chimneys, old Father Christmas,
White roofs, deep drooping trees
Like white clowns in a masquerade!

All's still—in one swoop ice bound!
In fur caps pulled down to the eyes,
Like wolverines creeping in trees,
They peer through the branches at me.

On my guard, I move through the snows.
The path dives adown a ravine—
To a vaulted chamber of hoarfrost,
To a door of branching small grills.

Behind a thick curtain of snow
Looms a shrouded, unusual lodge—
Near a trail to a lonely copse,
To a lonelier marvelous grove.

So majestic the stillness around,
Like a masterpiece fashioned in wood,
Like the lines of a quatrain about
A princess asleep in her tomb.

In this kingdom as quiet as death,
In my awe I quietly whisper
My thanks: O blessed Thy gift!
Thou givest far more than I ask.

1941

A Sentimental Waltz

I love her to tears, at sight, from the first,
As she comes from the woods—in storm and snow.
So awkward her branches, the shyest of firs!
We fashion her threads unhurriedly, slow,
Her garments of silvery gossamer lace,
Patterns of tinsel, and spangles aglow
From branch unto branch adown to the base.

We dress her in gold, the happiest fir!
So modest, aloof, her manner and air,
You will never forget, no matter where,
Her bluish enamel, her lilac foil.
I love her to tears, at sight, from the first,
As she is—in cobwebs—fresh from the soil.

We pin up her flags, we try on a star,
Range boxes of candy and wine in a jar,
Range candles about to grace her dear name,
Her fanciful make-up in light. Delighted,
She's much like an actress,—proud, excited,
Awaiting her cue to rise unto fame.
I love her to tears, from the first, so bright
In a crowd of friends on Christmas night.

Red apples to appletrees, cones unto firs.
But no commoner she! All glory to her—
Our holiday fir, especially great,
Eternal, elected, marked out by fate.
Her name is a legend year after year;

Exalted her name in the infinite sphere:
Like a prophet ascending to deathless renown,
She lifts to the ceiling her shining crown.

I love her to tears, at sight, from the first,
From the hour we dreamed about Christmas firs!

1941

On Early Trains

This winter season of the year
I live near Moscow. Foul or fair
The day, in frost or snow, I go
By train to attend to my affairs.

I start at daybreak in good time
When there is not a speck of light,
And leave my creaking steps about
The quiet woodland trails of night.

Before me at the railway crossing
White willows on a barren rise;
The constellations flame on high
In gulfs of January skies.

Always ahead of me, on time,
The mail train and express arrive,
Or Number Forty overtakes me,
Before I catch six twenty-five.

Sly wrinkles of dim light appear
Like feelers on a trembling stream
Of dark; the viaducts are stunned
By headlights in a sudden beam.

Inside the stuffy coach, seated
Among the plain and lowliest,
I fear I yield myself to feelings
I sucked in at my mother's breast.

But, brooding over past reverses
And years of our penury and war,
In silence I discern my people's
Incomparable traits once more.

And, worshipful, I humbly watch
Old peasant women, Muscovites,
Plain artisans, plain laborers,
Young students, and suburbanites.

I see no traces of subjection
Born of unhappiness, dismay,
Or want. They bear their daily trials
Like masters who have come to stay.

Disposed in every sort of posture,
In little knots, in quiet nooks,
The children and the young sit still,
Engrossed, like experts, reading books.

Then Moscow greets us in a mist
Of darkness turning silver-grey
When, leaving the underground station,
We come into the light of day.

And crowding to the exits, going
Their way, our youth and future spread
The freshness of muskcherry soap
And the smell of honeyed gingerbread.

1941

Thrushes

Far at a lonely country station
Deep silence falls on noontime plains.
Close by the railway line, goldfinches
Sing drowsily in dreamful lanes.

Sultry and boundless as desire,
The highway stretches far in space.
A lilac woodland glows beneath
A forelock of the cloud's grey face.

Along the wooded road the trees
Wave to the plodding horse in play.
Among the rotting stumps, in hollows,
Lie violets, leaf mould, decay.

No doubt the thirsting thrushes come
To drink in hollows such as these
When loud they sing the daylong tidings
With ice and passion in their knees.

In shrilling warnings long or short,
With trilling passionate or cold,
Their brass-lined singing throats are glossy
With puddles of the leafy mould.

They have their knolls and sheltered nooks,
Sly games of peeping through the blinds,
Their rowdy romps around the corners,
Their chatter, feuds about their finds.

Daylong throughout their airy chambers
Their secrets flash in public rhyme.
Dark copses quaver long their chorus,
And branches sing in quarter-time.

Such is the thrushes' shady haunt.
They live in nature's wood and brake,
Untamed, as every artist should,
And theirs the way I also take.

1941

The Tragic Story

A change will come. The capital,
Rebuilt, will live again.
But be forever unforgiven
The children's fear and pain!

There's no forgiveness for that fear
In faces seared and old.
For all its crimes the enemy
Shall pay a hundredfold.

We will remember cannonades,
And to the end condemn
The doers of the evil deeds
Like Herod in Bethlehem.

This age will pass. A brighter day
Will dawn, a time of peace.
But the woes of children maimed in wars
Live across the centuries.

1941

The Conqueror

Remember the dryness in the mouth
When, faced by a show of naked power,
We heard their savage bellowing,
And suffered in our trying hour.

But greater far than might of armor,
Our cause of human right and good,
The fate incarnate in Leningrad:
A wall before the world she stood.

Remember our great deliverance,
The break in the besiegers' base!
The world upon her ramparts gazed,
In wonder gazed upon her face.

She bore on land and in the skies
The wars to death, in agony.
How bright her legendary fame,
Her day of immortal destiny!

1944

Spring 1944

I shall never see a sweeter spring!
The sparrows are livelier and gay.
I do not even try to know
Why I am calm and glad today.

I work with a serener mind.
I hear the voice of liberty
In mighty octaves ring in choirs
From all the war-torn lands set free.

This tide of spring across the plains
Wipes clean away all winter traces,
And washes off the tears of care
And suffering in Slavic faces.

The grasses, panting, wait to burst
In light, and though the crooked alleys
Of Prague are still as graves, they too
Will sing like all the fields and gullies.

The soul of Czech and Serbian lands
Will wake with springtime tenderness,
And burst with flowers in the snow
Through shrouds of winter lawlessness.

Our fairy tales, long veiled in mist,
Revive like legends famed in story,
Portrayed in golden boyar chambers
And in Saint Basil's church of glory.

Our seers and dreamers in the night
Hold Moscow as their dearest home,
Their hope of good, the fountainhead
Of a noble century to come.

1944

THE POEMS OF
DOCTOR ZHIVAGO

Hamlet

The plaudits slowly die away.
Again I come upon the stage.
I strain to hear in dying echoes
The fate that waits our present age.

Through thousands of binoculars
The night of darkness stares at me.
If possible, O Abba, Father,
Then take away this cup from me.

I love Thy stern design, and I am
Content to act this role of woe.
But there's another play on stage;
Then spare me now, and let me go.

The acts are plotted, planned with care;
The end, foredoomed. I stand alone.
The Pharisees exult in pride.
O hard this life—our ways of stone.

March

The earth is steaming, drenched in sweat;
Ravines run dazed and turbulent.
Like a bustling milkmaid hard at work,
Spring labors long, is well content.

The scanty snows now sick and helpless
Lie prone, with branching bluish veins.
The tines of pitchforks glow with health,
Freed from their winter rust and stains.

O nights, O passing days and nights!
The drip from eaves and window sills,
The thinning icicles on gables,
The chatter of unsleeping rills!

The pigeons peck at oats in snow
About the barns and stables flung
Wide open, and vaster than spring air,
The smell of life-begetting dung.

Holy Week

The dark of night lies everywhere.
So young the night around,
We see how vast with stars the sky,
Each star as radiant as day.
And if the earth could have its way,
It would sleep on—through Easter Day—
Lulled by the reading of the psalms.

The dark of night lies everywhere.
So young the night, the square seems like
Eternity from end to end
Where still a thousand years must wait
The dawn of day and light.

The earth is naked to the bone:
It hasn't got a thread to wear
For swinging church bells in the night
Or singing with the choir.

From Maundy Thursday right up to
The eve of Easter Day,
The waters gnaw at riverbanks
And spin the waves in pools.

The woods are also naked,
And hushed through Passiontide;
The trunks stand crowded in a throng
Like worshippers at prayer.

And in the city, gathered near
The square, the thronging trees
Stand mother-naked too, and peer
Through gratings at the church.

They gaze with awe, and their alarm
And fears are justified:
The gardens leave their boundaries,
Degrees and laws of life are rent—
For God is given to the grave.

They see the light at the royal gate,
The black pall, the tapers glowing,
And faces wet with tears.
They see the long procession starting
With Cross and Shroud,
And how two birches at the gate
Step aside to let them pass.

They move around the cloister walls
In crowds from curb to curb,
And bring into the church the spring,
The voices of the spring,
The heady fumes of spring,
The springtime of the year and air
Pungent as a holy wafer.

March scatters handfuls of the snow
Like alms among the lame,
As though a man stood in the portals
Holding the Ark, and opened it,
And gave its all unto the poor.

They sing and pray until the sunrise.
And having wept their fill,
Their chanting of the Psalms and Gospels
Flows with an air serene
Into an empty lamplit street.

All creatures hear the voice of spring
In the still of night, believing
That when better weather comes
Death itself shall be destroyed
By the travail of the Resurrection.

White Night

I dream of a night long ago
And a house on the Petersburg Quai.
A poor landowner's daughter, you came
As a student alone to the city.

You were comely, admired by many,
So many. You and I, that evening,
Sit snug at your window, watching
The street from your attic room.

There lamps like butterflies flicker
In the chill of morning rays.
I speak to you softly—of matters
Still at rest in far-away time.

We dream we are bound together
By a feeling of timid devotion
To a mystery that holds our city
On the shores of the boundless Neva.

We hear, far among dark copses
In the silvery evening of spring,
The nightingales trill and whistle
Triumphant in revels of song.

The song of each singer, the frenzy
Of tremulous chirping and trilling
Awakens delight and unrest
In the depths of spell-bound groves.

And Night, like a barefoot pilgrim,
Secretly creeps by the fences,
Trailing behind her the wraith
Of our words from the window-sill.

In the cadence of echoing words
Overheard, in the gardens about,
The branches of apple and cherry
In shining white blossoms appear.

Like luminous phantoms the trees
Come thronging out on the highway—
To wave their farewell to Night
That knows what is fated to be.

Spring Floods

The sunset flames were dying down.
Along spring-flooded forest trails
A weary horseman made his way
To a lonely Ural mountain farm.

The horse came panting, all in sweat.
The churning streams along the road
Pursued the horseman, echoing
The swish and clink of hoofs in slush.

But when the rider dropped his reins
And slowed his horse down to a walk,
The spring floods thundered by his side
In all their gathered clash and roar.

There someone mocked, and someone wept.
Stone was ground to dust on stone.
The loosened and uprooted stumps
Tumbled into the swirling pools.

Against the sunset conflagration,
Among the charcoal branches flung
In space, the frenzied nightingale
Raged like a booming tocsin bell.

And where the weeping willow plunged
Her widow's veil above a hollow,
It whistled in the seven oaktrees
Like the Robber Nightingale of old.

What hopeless passion, what misfortune
Foretold this frenzied glowing song?
At whom the whistling singer aimed
This flying grapeshot in the woods?

It seemed that from a convicts' hide-out
A demon of the woods might rise
To meet the horse or foot patrols
Of partisans from local posts.

The earth and sky, the field and forest
Gave heed to each unique, fine tone,
Each measured note of sheerest madness,
Deep anguish, happiness, and pain.

Explanation

Life has returned, no matter how,
As once—no matter why—it snapped.
I live in the same old-fashioned street
As in that summer, on that day.

The folks the same; their cares, the same.
The sunset flames still faintly glow
Where the night of death had nailed them
Against the walls of Manege Square.

The women in cheap cotton dresses
Still saunter down the square at night,
And are, as then, still crucified
By attic rooms beneath tin roofs.

There one of them appears inside
Her doorway, dragging slow her feet,
Climbs slowly from her basement room,
And walks obliquely through the yard.

Again I'm ready with excuses
As one unmindful of the world.
I'm glad our next-door woman skirts
The alley, leaving us alone.

*   *   *

Oh, do not weep! Do not pucker
Your swollen lips again,
For that would only crack the scab
Made by the fevered spring.

Hands off my burning breast! We're like
Live wires; the current's on.
We shall again be thrown together
Unaware, against our will.

Yes, you will marry, then forget
The hardships of the past.
A woman's life is a noble quest
And trust—that drive men mad.

As for me, I've stood lifelong
A slave, in reverence
Before the miracle of woman—
Her throat, shoulders, hands.

No matter how the night may weld
Its chains of grief with longing new,
No power is fiercer than the passion
That pulls our lives apart.

Summer in the City

They whisper in silence.
With impetuous air
She sweeps up from her neck
Her tumbling hair.

Like a helmeted woman,
She peers out between
The encircling strands
That fall from her comb.

The night is seared
With its heat and grime.
The loiterers scamper
To get home on time.

From afar the thunder
Comes suddenly near,
And the window curtains
Flap trembling with fear.

Deep silence, The air is
Still muggy with heat;
Then flashes of lightning,
And scurrying feet.

When morning flames out
In a blaze again,
When the sun dries clean
The puddles of rain,

The lindens awaken
To a freshness deep,
Awaken sweet-scented
And heavy with sleep.

Winds

I have died. You live alone with woe.
Now stormwinds, keening and repining,
Rock house and pine trees to and fro—
Not tree by tree, but at one blow
All groves and forests intertwining
With the illimitable space;
Thus sailboats sheltered at their base
Are rocked by winds along a bay.
But not in senseless agitation
The stormwind rages day by day;
Of grief alone its lamentation,—
For you its lullaby of desolation.

Intoxication

Neath a willow with ivy entangled
We take cover in blustery weather.
My arms are wreathed about you;
In my raincape we huddle together.

I was wrong: Not ivy, my dear,
But hops encircle this willow.
Well then, let's spread in its shelter
My cape for a rug and a pillow.

False Summer

The leaves of the currants are woody.
Amid laughter and clatter of jars,
The women are shredding and pickling
With pepper and cloves for the winter.

Like a jester, the copse hurls headlong
Its hubbub far down a cliff
Where the hazels lie scorched in the sun
As if seared by ravaging flames.

A path runs down to the hollow
Where, among dry stumps and snags,
You feel sorry for Autumn, who sweeps
To the gully old rubbish and scrap;

Sorry too that creation is simpler
Than some clever chatterers think;
That the copses are sunk in morasses,
And that everything's fated to die;

That there is no sense in your staring
Because nature is shriveled by heat,
That the gossamer threads of Autumn
Drift in as ash through the windows.

There's a hole in the garden fence
And a trail to a copse of birches.
There's laughter and noise in the house,
Like the hubbub far down the cliff.

The Wedding Party

Many guests at evening came
To the wedding feast
For the marriage songs and dancing
Nightlong in the yard.

After midnight until seven
From the wedded couple
Not a whisper reached the crowd
Through their bedroom door.

But at early dawn when sleep is
Sweet with dreaming, dreaming,
The accordion sang out again
At the parting hour.

The harmonicas played loudly
One more merry tune
To the clapping and the stamping
Of the dancing guests.

Then again, again the ringing
Snatches of gay song
Burst upon the sleepers' bed
From the merrymakers.

There a wench, as white as snow,
Like a peahen glided,
Softly swaying, while the dancers
Whistled, whooped, and yelled.

Tossing jauntily her head
And her right hand waving,
Like a peahen, like a peahen,
Trippingly she went.

Suddenly all noise and shouting
And the swing of song
Faded into silence—faded
With the dying night.

Soon the yard became alive
With the rush of chores,
With their busy morning chatter
And their peals of laughter.

In a whirlwind of gray patches
Flocks of pigeons rose,
Soaring high above the dovecotes
In the boundless blue.

Surely someone, on awaking,
Came to set them free
As a greeting to the wedded,
As a good-luck wish.

Life is thus a moment only,
Only a dissolving
Of ourselves in other selves
As a gift to them.

Life is but a wedding gift
Bursting into light,
Like a song, a dream, a pigeon
Winging in the blue.

Autumn

I've given leave to all those dear
And near to me to go their way.
The world is empty; in my heart
I feel my lifelong loneliness.

We are together in this lodge,
Alone. The forest is deserted.
As in our ancient songs, the trails
Run wild in brambles and in weeds.

The timbered walls in quiet sadness
Regard both you and me. We made
No vows to leap all obstacles,
And thus we simply wait our end.

We meet at one—I with a book,
And you with your embroidery;
We shall not know at break of day
How long our kissing in the night.

Let leaves spin headlong down, ablaze
In glory, splendid in their death,
And swell our cup of bitter grief
With pain increasing day by day.

Let stormwinds strew as leaves afar
Our life, devotion, beauty, joy!
Like a leaf, my dearest, drift away,
Go half insane, out, out of sight!

Yet as the coppice flings its leaves
Upon the air, you loose your dress,
And in your silken dressing-gown
You fall into my waiting arms.

You are my gift of life when days
Grow baneful, worse than the disease;
But courage is the very root of beauty,
And it draws together you and me.

A Fairy Tale

Once upon a time
In a wonderland
A knight made his way
Through a barren steppe.

As he sped to battle,
He beheld a forest
Loom afar in space
In the heaving dust.

A foreboding clutched
His troubled heart:
Make tight the saddle!
Shun the water hole!

But the fearless knight
Spurned the warning voice
As he rode full speed
Up the wooded hill;

Then across a meadow
To a dried-up stream,
Then around a hill
To a narrow valley;

Through a murky hollow,
By a forest trail
He came at noontide
To the water hole.

Deaf to every fear
And the warning voice,

Down a steep he led
His thirsting horse.

*   *   *

By the winding stream
Across the shallow
Eerie flames sprang high
Above a yawning cave.

Through blinding smoke
And brimstone flames
A shrill cry rang out
Within towering pines.

The rider, startled,
Pressed bravely on
Through a long ravine—
Toward the call for help.

He beheld the dragon
And he gripped his lance;
He beheld its head,
Its tail, and scales.

The dragon darted
Red shafts of flame.
In three coils it circled
A maiden form.

The serpent's neck
Swung like a whip
Across the victim's
Head and shoulders.

Every year by custom
To that forest monster
Was sacrificed
A maiden's life.

This was the tribute
The people had to pay
To save their homes
From the serpent's wrath.

The dragon encircled
Her arms and throat—
She, men's tribute
And their sacrifice.

The knight lifted up
A prayer to heaven,
And he couched his lance
For the bitter fight.

*   *   *

Eyes shut in darkness.
High mountains. Clouds.
Fords. Waters. Rivers.
Centuries and years.

The knight fell wounded
On the bloody ground.
His charger trampled
The serpent in the dust.

There horse and dragon
Side by side lay dead;

The knight—unconscious,
The maid—in a trance.

The noontide skies
Shone soft and blue.
Who was she? A princess,
Or a peasant maid?

Her tears ran streaming
From excess of joy,
But she sank again
In a trance of sleep.

Then the knight awakened,
Too weak to move,
From his waste of strength,
From the loss of blood.

Their hearts were beating
As by swelling waves;
They sank, or wakened—
Only to sleep again.

Eyes shut in darkness.
High mountains. Clouds.
Fords. Waters. Rivers.
Centuries and years.

August

As promised free and faithfully,
The sun spread wide its morning rays
Abroad, and traced a saffron streak
From window curtains to my couch.

It spattered with its sultry ochre
The village cottages, the grove
Near by, my bed, my wet pillow,
The bookshelf, and a bit of wall.

I then remembered why my pillow
Had been so dampened with my tears.
I dreamed you came for a last farewell;
You trailed behind me in the woods

In groups, asunder, and in pairs;
That someone in the crowd recalled
It was the holy sixth of August,
The Lord's Transfiguration;

That on this day Mount Tabor shines
In clear pure light without a flame;
That, as an oriflamme in brightness,
Autumn entices every heart.

You came through the beggared scrub,
Through sparse and stunted alder trees,
Then reached the coppice and the church
Bright-flaring as a ginger bunny.

The sky was like a next-door neighbor,
Sedate above unruffled treetops,
And far away the air sang long
Of roosters interchanging calls.

Death hovered like a state surveyor
Inside the cloistered graveyard, scanning
Reflectively my dull dead face—
How best to dig my grave to size.

Each one, in every sense and feeling,
Heard inwardly my quiet voice,
My prophetic voice of days ago
That rang unsullied by corruption:

"Farewell, O skies of Transfiguration,
O gold of the Second Coming! Incline
To ease my grief in this fateful hour
With a last, a womanly caress.

"Farewell, O days of dull despair!
O woman, challenging all wrongs
And degradation, now we part!
It is I who was your battlefield!

"Farewell, O winged imagination,
And daring flights in life made free,
And worlds made manifest in words,
In thought, in miracles of art."

Winter Night

The snow was falling soft and slow
From land to land.
A candle flamed upon a table;
A candle flamed.

As midges of the summer swarm
Against a candle flame,
Outside the snowflakes swarmed against
The windowpane.

The blizzard modelled on the glass
White stars and arrows.
A candle flamed upon a table;
A candle flamed.

And soft along the lighted ceiling
Shadows lingered:
Shadows of crossed arms, crossed legs,
Crossed destinies.

Two little shoes fell to the floor,
Fell with a thud.
And soft the candle shed wax tears
Upon a dress.

The world lay soundless deep in snow,
Within a grey-white mist.
A candle flamed upon a table;
A candle flamed.

A draft then shuddered in the flame.
The fever of temptation
Raised up the cross of angel wings
Upon a wall.

Day after day through February
The snow came down.
A candle flamed upon a table;
A candle flamed.

Parting

He stands and stares across the hall
And does not know his home.
Her sudden leaving was a flight,
With chaos left behind.

He does not try to comprehend
The chaos in the room,
Because his headache makes him faint,
And tears make dim his eyes.

A throbbing pain rings in his ears.
Is he awake or dreaming?
And why so constant in his mind
The vision of the sea?

When you no longer see the world
Behind hoar-frosted panes,
The hopelessness of sorrow seems
Far greater than the lonely sea.

And yet he drew her close to him,
One dear in every feature,
As the shore is closer to the sea
With each inflowing tide.

As reeds sink downward in a storm
With seas in agitation,
Her graceful air and traits sank deep
Within his secret soul.

Through many years of trial, days
Of utmost wretchedness,
Borne up by a tide of destiny,
She reached to him for help.

Amidst the endless obstacles
And perils of the sea,
The waves had borne her on, but near,
And nearer to him still.

And now her sudden flight—perhaps
Not by her choice at all.
This parting may bring on new grief
And suffering unto death.

He looks around this room again.
In the hurry of her leaving,
She turned each old familiar thing
In every drawer upside down.

He paces up and down in darkness,
He stoops, keeps putting back
The scattered scraps of careful sewing
And patterns in their places.

And having pricked his finger on
A needle in the cloth,
He sees the whole of her in life
And weeps in silence, softly.

Meeting

The snow will bury roads
And houses to the roofs.
If I go to stretch my legs,
I see you at my door.

In a light fall coat, alone,
Without overshoes or hat,
You try to keep your calm,
Sucking your snow-wet lips.

The trees and fences draw
Far back into the gloom.
You watch the street alone
Within the falling snow.

Your scarf hangs wet with snow,
Your collar and your sleeves,
And stars of melted flakes
Gleam dewy in your hair.

By the light of flaxen braids
I see your face, your scarf,
Your shape alone in the cold,
In that thin overcoat.

Flakes gleam beneath your lashes,
And sorrow in your eyes.
You were created whole,
A seamless shape of love.

It seems as if your image
Drawn fine with pointed steel
Is now in silver lines
Cut deep upon my heart.

Forever there your mind,
Your true humility.
It does not really matter
If the world is hard as stone.

I feel I am your double,
Like you outside, in dark.
I cannot draw the line
Dividing you from me.

For who are we, and whence,
If their idle talk alone
Lives long in aftertime
When we no longer live?

Star of the Nativity

It was wintertime.
The wind blew hard from the plain.
And the infant was cold in the cave
On the slope of a hill.

He was warmed by the breath of an ox.
The cattle huddled
Within the cave.
A warm mist drifted over the manger.

On a cliff, far-off, the shepherds awoke,
Shook off the wisps of straw
And hayseed of their beds,
And sleepily gazed in the vastness of night.

They beheld the fields in drifted snows,
Gravestones and fences,
The shafts of a cart,
And a sky of stars above the graveyard;

And near them, unseen until then,
Like a watchman's candle
One star alone and shy
That shone on the road to Bethlehem.

At times it looked like a hayrick aflame,
Apart from God and the sky;
Like a barn on fire,
Like a farmstead ablaze in the night.

It reared in the sky like a flaming stack
Of straw and hay,
In the midst of all Creation
Surprised by this new star in the world.

And the flame grew steadily wider,
Large as a portent.
Then three stargazers
Hastened to follow the marvellous light.

Behind them, their camels with gifts.
Their caparisoned asses, each one smaller
In size, came daintily down the hillside.

And all new matters that were to come after
Arose as a vision of wonder in space.
All thoughts of ages, all dreams, new worlds,
All the future of galleries and of museums,
All the games of fairies, works of inventors,
And the yule trees, and the dreams all children dream:
The tremulous glow of candles in rows,
The gold and silver of angels and globes
(*A wind blew, raging, long from the plain*),
And the splendor of tinsel and toys under trees.

A part of the pond lay hidden by alders;
A part could be seen afar from the cliff
Where rooks were nesting among the treetops.
The shepherds could see each ass and camel
Trudging its way by the water mill.
"Let us go and worship the miracle,"
They said, and belted their sheepskin coats.

Their bodies grew warm, walking through snows.
There were footprints that glinted like mica
Across bright fields, on the way to the inn.
But the dogs on seeing the tracks in starshine
Growled loud in anger as if at a flame.

The frosty night was like a fairy tale.
And phantoms from mountain ridges in snows
Invisibly came to walk in the crowd.
The dogs grew fearful of ghosts around
And huddled beside the shepherd lads.

Across these valleys and mountain roads,
Unbodied, unseen by mortal eyes,
A heavenly host appeared in the throng,
And each footprint gleamed as an angel's foot.

At dawn the cedars lifted their heads.
A multitude gathered around the cave.
"Who are ye?" said Mary. They spoke: "We come
As shepherds of flocks, as envoys of heaven;
In praise of the Child and thy glory we come."
"There's no room in the cave; wait here a while."

Before dawnlight, in gloom, in ashen dark,
The drivers and shepherds stamped in the cold.
The footmen quarreled with mounted men;
Beside the well and the water trough
The asses brayed and the camels bellowed.

The dawn! It swept the last of the stars
Like grains of dust from the vaulted sky.

Then Mary allowed the Magi alone
To enter the cleft of the mountainside.

He slept in His manger in radiant light,
As a moonbeam sleeps in a hollow tree.
The breath of the ox and the ass kept warm
His hands and feet in the cold of night.

The Magi remained in the twilight cave;
They whispered softly, groping for words.
Then someone in darkness touched the arm
Of one near the manger, to move him aside:
Behold, like a guest above the threshold,
The Star of the Nativity gazed upon the Virgin.

Dawn

You were all my life, my destiny.
Then came the war and ruin, too,
And for a long, long time I had
No word, no scrap of news from you.

Now after many, many years
Your voice stirs memories of pain.
All night I read your testament,
And rouse myself to life again.

I long to be with people, crowds,
To share their morning animation,
Prepared to bring them to their knees,
To smash their fears and desolation.

And so each morning I run down
The stairs, at breakneck speed below,
As though this were my first release
To long deserted streets in snow.

The lights come on in cozy rooms.
Men drink their tea, and hurry down
To trolley lines. Within an hour
You'd hardly recognize the town.

The snows are falling thick and low
In silver nets above the street.
Men hurry on to get to work
And hardly take their time to eat.

My heart goes out to each and all,
To everyone who feels he's down;
I melt myself as melts the snow,
And as the morning frowns, I frown.

As wives, as children, or as trees,
The nameless are a part of me.
They rule my life, and by that sign
I know my sole true victory.

The Miracle

He walked to Jerusalem from Bethany
With forebodings and grief in His heart.

The thorny scrubwood lay scorched by the sun.
No smoke from a hut or hostelry near;
No breeze in the reeds. And the air was hot
And moveless by the glassy, quiet Dead Sea.

With a few small clouds in fellowship,
He wearily walked in the dust of day
With bitter sorrow as of the bitter sea
To be with His own desciples again.

So deep in loneliness, brooding, He moved.
The desert smelled in sadness of wormwood.
The world lay still. He stood in the midst
Of the desert alone. The land lay prostrate
As though in a faint. The heat, the desert,
Dry springs, and lizards wearied His mind.

He beheld a fig tree rise in the way,
With branches and leaves, but He found no fruit.
And He said unto it: "Of what profit thou?
What joy can I have in thy fruitless life?

"I thirst and hunger, but thou art barren.
Thy greeting is worse than stumbling on stone.
How empty, how senseless thy life in my sight!
Stay barren forever to the end of time."

A shudder ran down the tree at that curse,
As a spark of lightning runs down a rod.
And the fig tree instantly withered to ash.

But if roots and trunk, if branches and leaves
Had had their freedom and choice at that hour,
Then nature's laws might have come to their aid.

But a miracle is a sign—an act of God.
In days of confusion, when most we stray,
We stand, unprepared, before God our Lord.

Earth

Spring rushes like a roaring tide
By force into each Moscow home.
The moths come fluttering from closets
And settle into summer clothes.
The furs are packed away in trunks.

Along the wooden balconies
Bright flowerpots appear in rows
Showing off their gillyflowers.
Rooms have the free-and-easy look
Of spring, and attics smell of dust.

The alleys shout hail-fellow greetings
To every mole-eyed window frame.
White night and sunset by the river
Just cannot keep apart in passing.

And you can hear in every hallway
What's going on all day outside,
Or overhear gay April gossip
In secret with the dripping eaves.
He knows a thousand, thousand stories
About plain people and their sorrows.
Sunrise and evening red grow cold
Along the fence, while still they talk.

There is the selfsame eeriness
And heat in streets and living rooms;
Even the air seems not the same.

The selfsame lacy willow twigs,
The selfsame burgeoning white buds
At crossroads, under window sills,
In workshops, and in sunny streets.

Then why do the vistas weep in mists?
Why bitter the smell of soil and dung?
But that's just what my mission's for—
To keep the great outdoors from boredom,
And lands beyond the city bounds
From grieving in their loneliness.

That's why in early spring my friends
And I foregather in the night,
Why parting brings a sadness on,
Why friendly feasts are testaments—
That the secret stream of suffering
May warm the cold of earthly life.

Evil Days

When He came to Jerusalem
In the week before the feast,
He was hailed by loud hosannas,
And with palms unto His glory.

But days grew frightful and savage;
Men's eyebrows knit with disdain,
Their spirits unmoved by compassion.
And now the evil end.

The heavens lay heavy as lead,
With heaviness crushing the houses.
The Pharisees came after proof,
And wheedled like sly old foxes.

He was thrown to the scum by forces
Of evil supporting the Temple.
With the selfsame zeal they had lauded
His name, they cursed Him at last.

The rabble from the neighborhood
Gathered to peer in the gateways;
They jostled forward and backwards
And waited for the end to come.

The alleys whispered their rumors,
And the squares their secret talk.
He remembered the flight to Egypt
And His childhood as if in a dream.

He remembered the silent desert,
The majestic mountain top
Where Satan had tempted Him
With the kingdoms of the world.

And the marriage feast at Cana,
And the guests who gazed in awe,
And the sea whereon He had walked
To the boat as along dry land.

And the poor who met in a hovel,
His descent to the cave with a light;
How, frightened, the candle fluttered
When Lazarus rose from the dead.

Mary Magdalene

I

As soon as night descends, my demon
Walks right beside me. That is the price
I must pay for all my evil days.
Dark memories tear me then to pieces
When I, a slave to the whims of men,
Lived like a fiend, a wanton fool,
Whose only shelter was the street.

I have but a few scant minutes left
Before the silence of the grave,
Before the end. But while there's time
I shatter at Thy feet my life
As a precious alabaster vessel.

Oh, what would my existence mean
To me, O Master, O my Saviour,
If eternal life were not the life
Awaiting me at my table at night,
Like a late new visitor allured
Into the net of my profession.

But do make plain to me the truths
Of sin and death, hell, brimstone fire,
If I have grace, if I have come
To be through faith a part of Thee,
Even as branch and tree, when now
My heart is infinite with grief.

When I embrace Thy feet, O Jesus,
When dear I hold them in my lap,
I feel I am learning to embrace
At death the wooden beam, Thy Cross,
And, fainting, in my grief prepare
Thy body for the burial.

Mary Magdalene

II

Come spring, the women folk clean house,
Preparing for the holy Feast.
With myrrh, aloof from everyone,
I will anoint Thy most pure feet.

I'm looking everywhere to find
Thy sandals. I'm blinded by my tears.
My hair has fallen like a pall
In loosened coils before my eyes.

I have set Thy feet upon my lap
And washed them, Jesus, in my tears.
I wound my necklace round Thy feet;
I dried, I hid them in my hair.

I see the future clear, as though
The years stand still by Thy command,
And I can prophesy events
Like ancient sibyls in a trance.

The veil will tremble in the Temple,
While we will huddle, wait in fear.
The earth will rock under our feet,
Perhaps out of pity just for me.

The watchmen will be changed again,
And soldiers will be riding forth.

A whirlwind, springing in a storm,
Thy Cross will strive to reach the sky.

I shall lie prostrate, faint before
The Crucifix, and bite my lips.
Thy arms, O Lord, upon the Cross
Embrace too many in the world.

For whom Thy life, Thy open arms,
For whom such agony, such power?
Are there so many souls to save,
So many hamlets, rivers, woods?

Three days of agony shall pass,
Three days in frightful emptiness,
But in my faith I shall behold
The day of Resurrection come.

Garden of Gethsemane

The turn along the road was shining bright
In the regardless glimmer of far-off stars.
The road circled around the Mount of Olives,
And lower, in the valley, the Kedron ran.

A narrow meadow steeply dipped halfway,
And at its end the Milky Way began.
The silvery grey olives, straining forth,
Appeared to stride upon the empty air.

Beyond the meadow was someone's garden plot.
He left His disciples by the stone wall, saying:
"My soul is very sorrowful, even to death;
Remain outside and keep the watch with me."

He had refused, at His free will, the power
To work miracles, to have dominion over life,
As though these powers were His only on loan,
And now He stood as mortal, even as a man.

The boundless space of night seemed as a span
Of non-existence and annihilation.
The universal sphere was like a soundless waste,
And only the garden spot was warm with life.

And, gazing far into the black abyss
All void, without beginning or an end,
He prayed, the while His body sweated blood,
"My Father, let this cup pass from me."

He eased His deathly weariness with prayer.
He left the garden. He came to His disciples.
He found them in the wayside grass, asleep,
Their eyes grown heavy and their bodies weak.

He wakened them: "To you God granted life
While I am in the world, yet you sprawl like dead.
Behold, the hour is at hand, and the Son of Man
Delivers Himself into the hands of sinners."

And while He spoke, there suddenly appeared
A throng of slaves, a mob of vagrant men,
With swords and torches, and Judas at their head
With a traitor's kiss upon his lips.

And Peter drew his sword and smote the ruffians;
He struck a servant down, cut off his ear.
But Jesus said: "Put up your sword again.
The way of life is not the way of steel.

"And do you think my Father could not send
In my defense His hosts of winged legions?
My enemies would flee before my face
And never harm a hair upon my head.

"Behold, the book of life is open at a page
Of greater price than the holies of the past.
The written words shall be fulfilled at last,
And let the future come into the world. Amen.

"The passing of an age is like a parable,
And in the passing it may burst in flame.
In the name of its awesome majesty I will,
In my voluntary passion, suffer death.

"I will suffer death and on the third day rise
Again. Like rafts descending on a river,
Like a caravan of sails, the centuries
Out of the night will come to my judgment seat."

WHEN THE SKIES CLEAR

In All My Ways

In all my ways I strive to find
The vital part—
In stirring quests, in work, pursuits
Of mind and heart.

The source and meaning of our days
That went before
I would explore down to their roots
And very core.

I'd grasp the threads of great events
And destinies,—
To live, to ponder, love, and blaze
Discoveries.

If I could speak, in part at least,
With true compassion,
I'd write a stanza then about
The traits of passion!

About its sins, misdeeds and crimes,
Pursuit, release,
The consequence of arms and hands,
Chance and caprice.

I'd speak about its principles,
Its laws and aims,
And then repeat the first initials
Of its many names.

Like garden plots my lines would run
In trembling aisles;
My linden trees would bloom in rows
And in single files.

I'd give my verse the scent of mint,
The roses' wonder,
The breath of meadows, sedge and hay,
The roll of thunder.

Thus long ago Chopin infused
In his études
The living spell of groves and tombs
And solitudes.

The play, the trials, and the triumphs
Of a mind aglow
Are like the flight of arrows straight
From a tense bow.

1956

Fame

It's unbefitting to be famous
And say fame elevates our souls;
It's unbefitting to trouble over
Your notes and manuscripts and rolls.

The way of art is self-surrender,
Not born of praise or great success.
How shameful when your name's a byword;
Your labor—vain and meaningless!

Oh, live! Not as pretenders live—
In emptiness, with many fears,
But give your heart to vast horizons
And hear the call of future years.

Censor the contents of your books,
Not your destiny. Deliberate
And mark the matter lying near
Your vital themes of life and fate.

Then pass into your deep seclusion,
A man alone and unespied,
As vanishes in evening mist
And sudden dark the countryside.

Another, step by step, will follow
After, and enter your retreat,
But you yourself must not prefer
Your victories to your defeat.

You must never violate your purpose
One jot, one atom, to survive.
But be alive—this only matters,
Alive, to the end of ends alive!

1956

The Soul

My soul, O gentle mourner
For all my friends in pain,
Thou art the graveyard of
The tortured and the slain.

Their bodies now embalming,
And weeping at their hearse,
With sobbing lyre and prayer
Thou mournest them in verse.

In this, our age too savage,
As our conscience manifest,
Be thou the burial-urn
Wherein their ashes rest.

Their sufferings have bowed
Thy head in grief and gloom,
In reek of mortuaries,
In dank sepulchral tombs.

My soul, O charnel house!
Like grinding stone on stone
They crush us to a pulp.
The terrors we have known!

Crush still my life as grist,
My forty years of toil,
My years of trial smother
Deep in the graveyard soil.

Eve

Tall trees rise at the water's edge.
The summer noonday from a hill
Nearby hurls clouds into the pond,
Like fishing nets cast wide at will.

The sky's as heavy as a dragnet.
In the pond's sky as in a snare
A crowd of bathers swim together:
Men, women, children, everywhere.

Then from the water five, six women
Come up beside a willow-tree,
And each wrings dry upon the sand
Her dripping swim-suit noiselessly.

Like writhing adders on the sand,
The knitted woolens curl and cling
As if the serpent and the tempter
Lie hidden there, coiled in a ring.

O woman, your air and glances
In no wise tease my eagerness.
You are a noose around my throat
With feeling tense and tenderness.

You were created as a rough draft,
Strange as a page or line to keep,
And, jokes and fairy tales apart,
Made from my rib, indeed, in sleep.

At once eluding my embrace,
My hands that hold you closer, dear,
You are my spirit's gasp of pain,
Yourself an elf of sudden fear.

1956

Without a Title

So meek, so touch-me-not—you,
Yet aflame tonight—and perverse.
I'll wall up your beauty, apart,
In my darkling chamber of verse.

Look round you at objects transformed
By the lampshade light—the hall,
This room, the edge of the window,
Our shadows and shapes on the wall.

You sit, with legs crossed like a Turk,
On the ottoman fully at ease.
In darkness or light, like a child
You reason—but only to please.

Your concern, a string of small beads
In your lap. . . . Your words are sincere,
Altogether frank, and naive;
Your features are sad and severe.

That *love* is a worn-out word,
I'll grant you. Another for you
I'll find, for your sake, in the world
If you wish, and name it for you.

Do your looks, your frowning reveal
Your feelings, what's precious and rare
In the secret mine of your heart?
Then why, all sad, do you stare?

1956

The Change

I once had feelings for the poor
From no ideal cause or care
For them, but only because their lives
Seemed less a flaunting vain affair.

Although I knew the lords of rank
And culture, how gracefully they spoke,
I was the foe of hangers-on
And friend of many homeless folk.

I've always tried to be a friend
To men who daily work and slave;
For this I had the good reward
Of being dubbed a scurvy knave.

Their loathsome, empty cellar rooms
And attics with no curtains hung
Were things that stared me in the face
In silence,—as inhuman, wrong.

But since our sterile age laid bare
Our gross corruption, and with sneers
Turned grief into a thing of shame,
I too am tainted by their fears.

To those in whom I'd placed my faith
And trust I'm wholly now untrue.
Man is my forfeiture and loss
Since each and all have lost him too.

Spring In the Forest

A desperate late blast of cold
Delays the thaw. The air is keen.
Spring days are loitering behind
And burst upon us unforeseen.

The cock preens lustily before
The hens, and stills them on the run.
The pinetree, turning to the south,
Again blinks gladly at the sun.

Although the meadows steam and stew
For many weeks ahead, like rust
The roads lie fettered by the ice
Beneath a shield of blackened crust.

Fir needles and decaying cones
Bestrew each forest trail and pool;
Among the woodland trees the sun
And water have their share of rule.

The skies of downy clouds above
The grimy puddles at their feet,
Stuck fast among the highest branches,
Rest motionless, immured by heat.

1956

July

A ghost is roaming through our cottage,
And flits across the attic floor.
A goblin roams about the rooms,
Along the ceiling, at the door.

He bobs up in his awkward manner
And gets in everybody's way;
He blows the napkins off the table;
He flutters in our shirts at play.

With muddy feet he rushes in
On gusts of wind along the hall;
As though it were a dancing-girl,
He whirls the curtain up the wall.

But who's that batty, trifling ninny,
That country ghost who dogs our ways?
No, he's our lodger of the summer,
Our freakish guest of summer days!

He makes our cottage his possession,
In fee, while he enjoys his rest,
July of country air and thunder—
July's our tenant, boarder, guest.

July that lugs about his person
The burr and dandelion fluff;
July that scampers through the windows
And chatters loudly in a huff!

That tomboy, that dishevelled sloven
Who smells of fennel, lime, and rye,
Of dung and mulches, beets and grasses,
That meadow-scented month—July!

1956

After Mushrooms

The highway. Ditches. Woods.
We wander off in light
After mushrooms, and we mark
The mileposts left and right.

We leave the open highway.
We scatter, ranging through
The forest gloom; we ramble
Ankle-deep in dew.

Through thickets deep in dark
The spears of sunlight rush
On brown and yellow mushrooms
Under every bramblebush.

They hide among the stumps
Where birds alight to rest,
And when we lose ourselves,
The shadows guide our quest.

So brief these autumn days
And sunset solitudes,
The twilight has no chance
To linger in the woods.

Our bags and baskets burst
With gathered stock before
We leave for home: pine mushrooms
Make almost half our store.

Behind our backs the dark
Still forest walls arise,
And, beautiful in death,
The day flames bright and dies.

1956

Stillness

Transfixed, the wood in sunlight glows.
Sunbeams in shafts of dust explode.
From here, they say, an elk steps slow
And lumbers to the branching road.

The trees are moveless, haunted, hushed.
The hollows and the tangled dell,
Though not defeated by the sun,
Are silenced by some kind of spell.

Their fright is real: In fact, an elk
Stands hidden, rooted in the brush.
The trees, dumbfounded, stare in fear—
That's why the wood is in a hush.

The elk is nibbling at young shoots
And seedlings on the grassy track.
An acorn dangles on a branch,
Trembling above its crested back.

The oxeyes, thistle, St.-John's-wort,
Rosebay, primrose, and camomile,
Entangled by their panic doom,
Stare long in every brushwood aisle.

One stream alone in the ravine
Of sound and balm, in wonderment,
Rehearses soft or loud in haste
The tale of that singular event.

It calls to woodmen in the lodges
Through sounding gorges of the wood,
And tries to tell the fateful news
In every human neighborhood.

Hayricks

Dragonflies flit in blazing darts,
And bumble-bees fly on all sides;
Farm girls halloo atop the wagons,
And reapers stride beneath their scythes.

And while the sunny weather holds,
They rake the fodder turning brown;
They stack it deftly into ricks,
Like houses, till the sun goes down.

Each rick in evening dusk assumes
The likeness of a lodging hut,
Where night lies down to rest upon
A bunk of clover freshly cut.

At break of day the hayricks loom
Like lofts in ashen morning light,
Where the harvest moon digs itself in
While stopping over for the night.

At early dawn cart after cart
Rolls creaking on in murky air.
In twilight fields, the day crawls out
Of bed with hayseed in its hair.

Again the sky shines blue, again
Ricks rise as clouds in the noon hour.
Like vodka steeped with aniseed,
The earth lies sweet and vast in power.

The Linden Avenue

A manor of uncommon beauty,
An arching gateway, solitude.
Set in a dark, cool park, it rules
Rich meadows, fields, a distant wood.

Beneath their dusky canopies
The ancient linden trees, like peers,
Commemorate in shady lanes
Their record of two hundred years.

Outside the lane of vaulted branches,
Along symmetric passages
Lie lawns and plotted flowerbeds
Gay in their summer gala dress.

No sunny patterns on the sands
Beneath the ancient trees attend
The dim long tunnel; only the exits
Gleam bright in daylight at each end.

But, in the time of blossoming,
The fenced-in trees as in a tent
Of pillared shadows spread about
An overpowering magic scent.

Here visitors, in summer dress,
While strolling in this wonderland,
Enjoy the unfathomable sweetness
Which bees alone can understand.

This gripping fragrance is the garden's
Great truth and essence if we look
For truth. The lawns and flowerbeds
Are like the covers of this book.

Like waxen candle-lights, the flowers
Transfiguring each linden tree,
Above the manor house flame bright
In leaping tongues of ecstasy.

Clear Skies Again

The lake is one enormous bowl.
The sky—a multitude of clouds
Like piles of mountain glaciers risen
Immovably in dazzling crowds.

In veering daytime light the woods
Seem new and changeful, not the same:
One moment deep in murky shadows,
On a sudden like a torch aflame.

When, after days of stormy weather,
Between the clouds looks out the vast
Blue sky, how festive in their triumph
The lowly grass and fields at last!

The winds lie still in calmer air;
The sun is kindred to the grass;
The leaves in light transparent glisten
Like figures etched in colored glass.

In the stained windows of the church
True prophet, saint, and holy wife
In shining crowns, unsleeping, keep
Their vigil with eternal life.

I feel the dim cathedral nave
Grow vaster, infinite with calm,
And hear far choirs in the spheres
Ring out in one triumphant psalm.

O World, O Life, immortal Time!
I will now in secret adoration
Live, trembling, faithful in your service
With tears of joy and exaltation.

1956

Bread

For decades you've treasured conclusions
But never expressed them on paper;
If you're not in spirit a cripple,
There's something you must understand.

You've grasped the pleasure of work,
The secret and laws of success;
You've learned the evil of idling,
And the joy of self-dedication;

That the mighty kingdom of beasts
And the sleepy kingdom of plants
Await their defenders, their heroes,
Their altars and new revelations;

That of all revelations, the first
Remains in the ranges of fate
As a gift from past generations—
The bread we've cherished for ages;

That fields of ripe wheat and rye
Still summon the reapers to reap;
That, moreover, this call in the past
Was your ancestor's message to you;

That such was his precept in life—
His true, unexampled beginning
In the movement of days and years,
And of birth and sorrow and death.

1956

Autumn Woods

The autumn wood turns hairy,
With calm and shadows deep;
No woodpecker, squirrel, owl,
Now wakes it from its sleep.

By autumn trails the sun
At twilight enters it,
Looks warily about
In fear of a snare or pit.

Here swamps and moss abound;
Here tangled alders glow.
Beyond the forest marshes
A cock begins to crow.

Again and again it crows,
Then stops for very long,
As though perplexed to know
The meaning of its song.

But soon another cock
In some far village yard
Takes on the challenger
Like a sentryman on guard.

Cock after cock sings loud
With still increasing zest,
Their outcries pointing north
Or south, then east or west.

The trees lean out to see
How wide the fields, how new
And vast the world beyond,
How infinite the blue.

First Frosts

One chilly morning when the sun,
A pillared flame in smoke, shone dim,
I too as in a blurred snapshot
Was hardly visible to him.

Until the sun comes out of dark
And lights the field beyond the lake,
The trees can hardly see me where
I stand upon the distant brake.

A man is recognized much later
When he vanishes in mist as lost.
The chill dim air, like rouge, deceives;
A film of gooseflesh shrouds the frost.

I walk along these hoarfrost trails
As across a muffled matted stretch.
The earth feels loathe to bear this cold
Or smell potatoes in a patch.

1956

Night Wind

Drunk songs and noise die away.
They must rise at dawn, they said.
All the lights go out. The lads
Have started for home and bed.

The wind reels about the village
Alone on the same wild track
Where before in a crowd of fellows
He wandered up, down, and back.

He droops in a doorway. He hates
The night-time wrangling and trouble;
He'd rather reach an agreement
With night and forget their squabble.

They collide by the garden hedges.
They quarrel and feud in the lane.
The trees on the highway debate
The cause of that quarrel again.

Golden Autumn

Autumn. Magic palace halls
Open to a world awake.
Vistas of long forest trails
Mirrored in the glassy lake.

Halls and halls, bright galleries
Hung with painted autumn views,—
Aspen, elm, the oak and ash
Glow in unimaginable hues.

There the golden bands of limes
Shine like garlands on a bride,
And the birch beneath her veils
Rises in her nuptial pride.

Meadows under bedded leaves;
Holes and ditches dank with mould.
Huts behind the yellow maples
Blaze aloft in frames of gold.

When the trees loom pair by pair
In the dawnlight of September,
Or the sunset lingers longer
On their bark in shining amber;

When ravines are loud with leaves,
Swarming in each glade and brake,
And the hosts of frenzied leaves
Noise abroad each step you take;

When the echoes ring on slopes
At the ending of a lane
Where, like the red-cherry gum,
Sunset skies blaze red and wane,—

Then it's autumn. Good old nooks,
Good old books and guns your treasure;
Frost is turning slow the pages
Of your catalogue of pleasure.

   1956

Foul Weather

The rain has mired the fields and roads.
The moaning winds cut pools like glass.
They strip the willow tresses down
And clip them closely as they pass.

A graveyard crowd go homeward slow.
Leaves flutter down to a dead stop.
A sweaty tractor, pulling hard
Eight harrows, ploughs the winter crop.

The leaves whirl down along the pond
And rest in furrows shining black;
Like ships maneuvering in line,
They sail across the rippling track.

Rain drizzles through a sieve of air;
The cold grips hard as in a brace.
The universe seems veiled in shame
As though this autumn spells disgrace.

The mingled flocks of leaves and crows,
The driving edges of the rain,
The hurricane that lashes blind,
Seem as our lasting shame and pain.

1956

Grass and Stones

So fused are stone and plant,
Illusion and reality
In Poland and in Georgia
That both are alike as twins.

As though Annunciation Day
Bestowed her springtime grace
From every creviced rock,
From grasses under walls:

A promise fulfilled by nature,
By the labor of busy hands,
By craftsmanship and science,
By each creative art;

By sprouting branch and leaf,
By earth in the smallest cleft,
By the ruins of centuries,
By grasses under walls;

By slothfulness, by striving,
By bursts of ravished speech,
By converse great in aims,
By chatter and vainer talk;

By fields of tallest wheat
Over-arching peasant heads,
By earth beneath stone footings,
And grass under rotted floors;

By fragrant flowering bushes
And vines of the centuries,
Entwining ancient greatness
And a loveliness to be;

By double lilac clusters
In their white and purple hues
Between glowing corridors
And walls of crumbling forts.

Where men are nature's kin,
And nature is kin with men,
Earth fills all stony places,
Grass springs at every door:

When Mickiéwicz's proud lyre
And the speech of Georgian queens
Become hallowed in the airs
Of courts and servants' halls.

1956

Night

Night sweeps immutably,
Dissolves in air, but still
The pilot weaves in clouds
Above the drowsy hill.

He's lost in streams of jet,
In whirls of mist and sleet,—
A dot in the woven night,
A mark on a linen sheet.

Lights of unknown cities
And all-night inns stand out,
Then power houses, barracks,
Stations and trains about.

The shadow of his wings
Falls flat upon the clouds.
The stellar bodies drift,
Huddle in swarming crowds.

With dreadful, dreadful yawing
The Milky Way swings far
To a universe unknown,
Some unfamiliar star.

In immeasurable spaces
The planets burn and bloom.
Men stoke unsleeping fires
In a basement boiler-room.

From under roofs of Paris
The blinking eyes of Mars
Or Venus peer at posters
That name the latest farce.

But someone keeps awake
In far-off velvet space.
He gazes from his attic
As from a hiding place.

He stares at stars as though
The heavens were aware
And troubled by his vigils
And themes of daylong care.

Work on, O watchman! Wake
And scant no work in sight.
Stay as a star or pilot
Unsleeping through the night.

Work on, O poet! Wake,
Arise in song and rhyme!
Immortal hostage you—
A prisoner of time!

1956

WIND
(Four Fragments About Blok)

1. Who Should Live

Who should live and be exalted,
Who censured, reviled, left out,
Such is the knowledge of rulers
And privileged toadies about.

They assume no man could know
Whether Pushkin is honored or not
Without their doctoral theses
To enlighten us all on the spot.

But Blok, thank God, is different,
So different in all his affairs!
He did not descend from Sinai
Or claim us by right as heirs.

Outside all schools and dogmas,
Eternal, alone, he stands—
His greatness above all systems,
His glory not builded by hands.

2. *He Is Like the Wind*

He is like the wind—like the wind
And storm in their country demesne
When Phil still rode in the lead
Of the family six-in-hand team.

The Jacobin grandfather Blok
Was a radical true and kind;
His grandson never did falter
Or slack by a jot behind.

The wind that struck to the heart,
In his spirit self-purified,
Was remembered for good and evil—
In his poetry glorified.

Wind everywhere—in the trees,
In villages, houses, rain,
In the verse of volume the third,
In *The Twelve*,—and in death again.

3. The Great Field

O wide in the sun the great field,
The field far away, and the stream!
We toil at the mowing together,
We reap, and we thresh as a team.

No time for reapers to loiter
And gaze at the riverside!
The mowing aroused young Blok,
The squire's son with his pride.
By mere luck he missed a hedgehog,
Hit a snake or two with his scythe.

The lad hadn't finished his lessons.
"Lazybones!" they gibed with a smirk.
O childhood! O wearisome schooldays!
O ditties of weeders at work!

A black cloud rolled up from the east
On a sudden in evening's hush.
A savage, unseasonal stormwind
Slashed reapers' scythes in its rush,
And, hurling itself on the stream,
Crushed bush and sedge into slush.

O ditties of weeders at work!
O childhood! O wearisome schooldays!
O wide in the sun the great field,
The field far away in a haze.

4. The Horizon's On Fire

The horizon's on fire with menace
And bruised by the dawnlight flood,
Like scores of bruises unhealed,
Like a reaper's feet in blood.

No end to rents in the sky,
Forerunners of storms and defeat.
O the reek and rust of swamps
In the air, and death in the street!

In forests, highways, ravines,
In villages, cities of dearth,
The zigzagging clouds betoken
Hard times and trials on earth.

When over the capital city
The sky flares purple and rust,
A hurricane threatens the State,
The imperial center of lust.

Blok spoke at the dawn of strife.
He read in the sky the foreknown,
The fury of storms and tempests,
The terror, the frightful cyclone.

Blok awaited the storm and upheaval.
In the flame of his work and strife,
His doubts and fears of the issue
Sank deep in his verse and life.

1956

The Highway

Up hill, down hill and dale,
Round bend, or straight ahead,
The highway endlessly
Like a ribbon crooks and coils.

Redeemed from dust and mud,
Past wayside fields and woods
By laws of true perspective
The surfaced highway winds.

It spans the ancient dam
Without a sidelong glance
At a brood of ducklings
Swimming across the pond.

It speeds up hill, down hill,
To one appointed end
As life itself at times
Strives with one aim ahead.

Despite a thousand phantoms
Of time and place and days,
It masters obstacles
And speeds on toward its end.

At home or out, its aim's
To prove, endure, survive,
To quicken open spaces
And wake the countryside.

In the Hospital

They crowded, blocking the sidewalk
As before a window display;
They watched the stretcher uplifted
And the ambulance speed on its way.

Past houses, markets, and loungers
At corners, it shrilled in the night;
It hurled in confusion, in courses
Of darkness, two arrows of light.

Militiamen, crossings, and faces
Bobbed up in the light of the car;
The first-aid attendant was swaying
With her kit and ammonia jar.

The gutters drearily pattered
With rain at the entrance; the age
And the patient's case were scribbled
On line after line on a page.

He was left on a cot in the hall,
For the ward was full at that time.
The hall was drafty; the passage
Oppressive with iodine.

A window held bits of a garden,
A square of light and the sky.
He studied the beds and the sick
And the bustling attendants nearby,

When, catching a nurse's attention,
He suddenly knew in his pain
That the hospital wards would never
Return him to freedom again.

Thankful, he turned to the window
And faced a great wall outside
That reflected the lights of the city
In their changeful, smouldering tide.

The lights of the avenues glimmered
In the shuddering flames of the sky;
A branch of a maple in tatters
Was waving to bid him goodbye.

"O Lord!" he sighed in his sorrow,
"How perfect the works of Thy hand!
The beds, the walls, my passing
In death, the night in the land.

"I swallow a sedative capsule;
I weep in my desolate place.
O Father, my tears and torments
Keep me from seeing Thy face!

"How sweet Thy light to my spirit,
At the end in my agony;
How sweet that my lot and being
Are Thy gift of life unto me.

"And, dying, I feel that Thy hands
Are ablaze, that I die in Thy grace,
That I rest, O Lord, in Thy keeping,
Like a priceless ring in a case."

1956

Music

The house loomed like a tower,
A belfry over thoroughfares;
Two huskies heaved a piano
Up winding narrow stairs.

Above a sea of streets
They lifted the piano high
As tables of the law
On stony Mount Sinai.

The piano and the room
Hear the boom and blare far down,
And deep as buried legends
The rumble of the town.

Upon his balcony, alone,
The sixth-floor tenant stands,
Like a man who holds the world
In rightful sovereign hands.

Inside, he shapes a forest
Or a High Mass with notes,—
No alien borrowed music
His chorales of inmost thoughts.

His impromptu bears the tumult,
The clatter of streets and lanes,
The fate of lonely hearts,
The night, the flames, and rains.

So Chopin at his music rack
By candles scored his dreams
And made the world forget
The time-worn simple themes.

Thus ahead of generations
Rode in a storm of hoofs
The Valkyrie in their flight
Across the city roofs.

Thus sad Chaikovsky moved
The halls to tears and shook
Men's hearts with Paolo,
Francesca, and their book.

1956

After the Interval

Three months or so ago
When storms from overseas
In their fury burst upon
Defenseless garden trees,

I fancied I could hide,
Play hermit by design,
And plan to fill a book
With poems of winter time.

But odds and ends piled up
Like snowdrifts in a mound;
My plan of work fell through,
Although my plan was sound.

At last I knew the reason
Why cold and winter storm
Had pierced the dark with snow
And spied me soon at home.

It whispered, pale with cold,
"O hurry!" But in my den
I parried with a jest
While playing with my pen.

I dawdled at my table
One morning, still content,
And missed to hear the message
As winter came and went.

First Snow

The snowstorm whirls in swarming flakes
Shrouding one and all—
The paper stall and paper girl
Under a downy pall.

It seems, from long experience,
None will dare deny
The snow is born of secrecy
Only to mystify.

He tricks you out, sly reprobate,
Beneath a fringe of white,
And brings you from some frolic home
Late in the night.

While roads are blinded by the storm
And dazed with hoar,
A shadow staggers near the house,
Groping for the door.

It moves about unsteadily,
And for all I know
Someone has some misdeed to hide
Deep down in snow.

1956

Snows Are Falling

The snows are falling—falling low,
Whirling in the winter storm.
On window sills geraniums
Watch in amaze the starry swarm.

The snows are falling, hurry-scurry,
Round and about in tumbling flight,
On roofs and porches, trees and gates,
And paths zigzagging left and right.

The snows are falling, and it seems
Not merely snows are circling down,
But, mantled white, on spiral stairs
The sky's descending on the town.

Just like a harlequin or clown
From a steep landing in the air,
Playing hide-and seek, the sky
Comes stealing down a secret stair.

Because time does not stay or wait,
Before you turn around—it's Yule.
And with a little wink, behold
New Year again—the bountiful!

The snows are falling thick and low.
Do days go by—deliberate
And slow, in step with falling snows,
Or, in a flurry quite as great,
Whirl off like snowflakes in a storm?

Perhaps year follows year for ages,
Like dancing flakes of snow in space,
Like words across the poet's pages.

The snows are falling—falling low.
The snows are falling, hurry-scurry:
The flowers gaze in sheer delight
On paths zigzagging left and right
And passing folk as white as snow.

Footprints in the Snow

Across the snowfields slantingly
Felt-booted girls leave their trace,
From village to another village
To the red sunset far in space.

A sunbeam drips in holes and hollows
Like juice of lemon from a height,
And like a child stuck to its mother,
It chills to ice in pools of light.

Snow freezes like the dripping whites
Of eggs when broken in the shell,
And skis cris-cross it on their run
In lines of blue undaunted flight.

The moon like a pancake swims in cream;
It slithers sideways like a ball.
The speeding sleighs in mad pursuit
Will never catch the scudding ball.

After the Blizzard

All night the storm raged on. At dawn
The earth lay calm as in a dream.
I love to hear the children shout
At play across the frozen stream.

Most likely I am all mistaken,
Crazed by the storm, or maybe blind,
When winter seems the plaster cast
Of a woman dead from frost and wind.

The sky's amazed to see a moulded
White figure lying dead below.
The yard, the barn, the bushes, fences,
Lie sheeted, buried deep in snow.

The river banks, the belt of groves,
Embankment, platform, and the rails
Are domes of rounded dazzling drifts
Beneath immaculate long veils.

I jump up sudden from my sofa,
Awake, inspired, and run to do
A universe of winter scenes
On paper in a stanza or two.

On sculptured stump and fallen tree,
On roofs and bushes I bestow
A world of meaning on a page—
My universe of sky and snow.

Bacchanalia

Moscow. A winter sky.
Arched gates. A murky night.
At the church of Boris-and-Gleb
The mass in evening light.

Bright chasubles. At prayer
Old men and kerchiefed dames,
Their faces dimly lighted
By waxen candle flames.

Outdoors the swirling storm
Blends all in snow and sleet;
Arm in arm no pair can walk
Across the icy street.

The howling winds in fury
Blot out the world in sight:
Homes, prisons, excavators,
And cranes on building sites.

Wisps of posted handbills
In the wind flap crazily.
The trees on boulevards
In silver filigree.

Signs of a surging era,
The hurry to and fro,—
In quickness of the crowds,
In tracks of tires on snow.

In lifted steady voices
We mark epochal signs:
Antennas, friendly smiles,
Brave talk, electric lines.

Plain dress and simplicity
In every home-bred art
Of moving words and thoughts
Make glad the human heart.

A life of greater meaning
Shines through their poverty
Beneath the double sign
Of loss and majesty.

II

Zim, *Ziss*, and *Tatra* cars
Sweep up in the night;
They blind the sidewalks
With a pageant of light.

Outside, in the blizzard,
With their offers of seats
Black-market dealers
Encumber the streets.

In their lines, in file,
Crowds jostle their way,
All eager to see
The *Mary Stuart* play.

The young bring passes
For specified tiers.
They greet their idol
With a blaze of cheers.

III

They scuffle for tickets
In the ante-room.
Stage sets and scenes
Arise through the gloom.

The Queen of Scots
Appears suddenly,
Like a dancer who leaves
Her own galaxy.

For freedom, her life,
Her anguish and pain;
Dark prison walls
And chains are in vain.

As gay as a gadfly
Her past of guile—
To tantalize men,
To snare with a smile.

For this cause, perhaps,
Like a flaming brand,
She is doomed to die
By the hangman's hand.

In her ashen dress
She sinks in a chair;
The footlights etch
Her skirt and hair.

All the same to her—
Coquette or star,—
Their stage, or verse,
Or Paris, Ronsard.

What matter at death
Their hatred and blame,
Home, forts, and moats,
The reflector's fllame?

Her heroic death,
Her flame sublime
Will grip all hearts
In the aftertime.

IV

What madness, daring, joy,
What anguish of the soul,
To fuse the role and actress,
The actress and the soul!

As though that tragedy
Across the years of pain
Allows a queen long dead
To slip her chains again.

How rare, indeed, the spirit,
The luck and fame how rare,
To play through the centuries
As plays the lambent air,

As rivers and as trees,
As wines, as diamonds play,
As one is called forever
Time after time to play,—

As the lass with braided hair,
Who wears a stripe on white,
Plays well to simple folk
Her fateful role each night.

V

Again in the street.
The blizzard sweeps on.
Lights shine in the church;
The service goes on.

Chill winter skies.
Winter holidays.
Under mounds of tinsel
Shop windows blaze.

At parties, feasts,
At a birthday spree,
Furcoats pell-mell
Sprawl casually.

Laughter, small talk,
Opinions of men;
Three baskets of lilac
And white cyclamen;

Rows of caviar,
Cheeses, dates,
Red salmon, salads
On purple plates.

Crackle of napkins;
The pungent spice;
All sorts of vodka
And wines on ice.

A hubbub of chat.
Bright chandeliers
Flood shoulders, busts,
Gold rings in the ears.

Like grapeshot the lips
That chatter at will:
Those heartless hands
And smiles of goodwill.

VI

Watching such marvels
A strange maniac,
In silence, till dawn
Imbibes cognac.

Some dunces deplore
The fellow's excess.
He's steady, in fact,
At his sixteenth glass.

Long regarded by some
As a mute specimen,
He's clever with women,
Unsocial with men.

Three times divorced
And grey ere his prime,
He excused the women
And the blankness of time.

He shared their gifts
Without any concern,
And freely bestowed
His own in return.

He'd stop at nothing,
No matter what cost,
For a gay young skirt
He fancied the most.

VII

A danseuse looked bored
By vodkas and gins;
He sat close beside her,
And they felt like twins.

She longed for applause
Among the elite,—
To die like a queen
Though minus a suite.

He moves to the stairs
With his queen beside,
For a breath of air
From the heat inside.

Cold air feels good
To a chrysanthemum;
He must take her back
To the stuffy room.

Dead stubs on tables
With candies, pies,
And ashes in teacups.
A new dawn in the skies.

To know her figure,
His slender danseuse,
He kneels on the floor
And laces her shoes.

They discover a special
Regard for each other,
A fondness like that
Of sister and brother.

Again at her home
He falls to his knees,
While portraits frown
On favors like these.

What matter their fears,
Or conscience, or shame,
When delirium rules
Their hands aflame?

One moment alone,
The passion, the flame,
Feels truer than life,
Feels dearer than fame.

VIII

Night flowers slumber so still at dawn
That bucketfuls of water can't wake
Their petals from their morning sleep.
Their ears alone will feel the roar,
Some fitful snatches of a 'phone
Repeated thirty times or more.
They slumber in their flower beds
Like captives of night fantasies;
All the unruly, shameful things
Have faded from their memories.

Earth essences are sound and pure.
To purge and purify the room,
A dozen roses in a vase
Without favor waft their sweet perfume.
Thus pass their nights away, routine
Good times, their sport and fun. . . .
The dishes, washed; the kitchen, clean. . . .
They live, unthinking, on the run.

Around the Turning

On the alert beside the wood's
Dim thoroughfare,
A small bird twitters on a bough
In evening air.

She sings and twitters in a trance
In leafy gloom,
On watch before the entrance to
Her forest home.

The clouds on high. Along the ground
Dead leaves in heaps.
In a ravine around the corner,
The springs and steeps.

Here rotted stumps and logs and snags
Lie widely strewn;
In oozy pools and chilly swamps
The snowdrops bloom.

But this small bird believes her song's
A pledge, an oath,
And wants no straggler near—to pass
The undergrowth.

Around the turning, in a ravine
Of denser sedge,
My future waits—a fate more sure
Than any pledge.

It waits unmoved by words of praise
Or raging feuds.
It ranges far and wide in space
Like pinetree woods.

1958

Fulfilment

The roads have turned to slush. I look
About for a footing firmer, drier.
I squash like dough the clay and ice
And wade in pools of sticky mire.

With shrilling cries a jay whirs by
Above the vacant birchen wood
That stands like an untenanted
Half-finished house in solitude.

Now through a clearing here in light,
My future stands revealed to me.
I mark the things that come to pass
Down to the very last degree.

I walk in the woods. I do not hurry.
The forest gladly gives me way.
The echo quickly answers me
Just as it answers to the jay.

Amid the slush of sodden clay
And thaws that show the bottoms bare,
A small bird twitters on the sly
With little stops and notes to spare.

The trees eavesdrop and bear the song
Of this live magic box from glade
To glade, repeat each echoing note,
Then wait a time for each to fade.

There, too, three miles away, I hear
Around my hut that stands aloof
The crunch of steps, the drip of trees,
The plop of snow from off the roof.

1958

Ploughing Time

So unfamiliar, new, this land!
Who can tell the fringe of skies revealed
From earth below? Like chessboard squares
Each furrowed and unbroken field.

The harrowed fields lie vast and trim
Spread level on the plains about
As though the valleys had been swept,
Or else the hillocks flattened out.

On these days, too, outside the furrows,
As one in mind, unitedly
The downy trees burst into leaf
And reach out skyward, tall and free.

No speck of dust on a single maple,
And nowhere are the hues as bright
And pure as those on silver birches,
Or on the fields in haze of light.

1958

The Journey

The train runs on with gathered speed.
Black locomotive wheels spin fast.
The pinewoods smell of sap and tar;
The birches climb the upward slopes.
But there's adventure still ahead.

The track runs on past poles beside,
Ruffling the girl conductor's curls.
The streaming air grows acrid, hot
From fumes that spread along the slopes.

The rage of cylinder and piston.
The flash of the connecting rod.
A hawk skims like a shadow high
Above the gleaming railway track.

The engine sighs, sighs deep in smoke
That hangs on like a rakish cap.
But as in the days of old King Cole,
In centuries and decades past,
The forest, heedless of our decade,
Stands dreaming still its ageless dream.

And somewhere, somewhere, on a crest,
A city looms remote in space
Where, weary, in suburban darkness,
The train pulls up at some old station
And casts its human cargo free.

The cities draw these humble people
Disgorged at station stops and yards,—
Plain passengers, caretakers, clerks,
Conductors, firemen, engineers.

With doubled secrecy and care
The train moves by the winding streets
Above elevated massive walls
And arches builded stone on stone.
Flags, posters, chimneys, balconies,
Hotels, shops, theatres, club rooms,
Green squares and parks and linden trees,
Apartments, lodgings, iron gates,
Wide archways, porticoes, and halls,
Where passions strive, intrigue, and dream
A man-made new-created world.

1958

Women In My Childhood

I recall from my childhood days
As I peered through an open window
That our lane was dark, like a quarry,
At midday under the trees.

Twin rows of poplars enclosed
Down the narrow lane, in their shade,
The roadway, sidewalks, basements,
And the church with its bulbous roof.

A pathway of grasses and weeds
Cut through a neglected garden.
The women who lived there imparted
A mysterious air to our lane.

The girls next door attracted
A bevy of tattlers and friends.
The fragrance of fresh muskcherry
Made sweet their casement windows.

There grownup quarrelsome women,
Worked up by their common abuse,
Stood cross in the doorways, like trees
That border municipal rosebeds.

I sulked, enduring in silence,
Their lashing tongues and twitter;
To love them became, like science,
An act of devotion and wonder.

To all I remember from childhood,
Like shadows of days long ago,
I say to them truly, "I thank you,"
Convinced I am still in their debt.

1958

The Passing Thunderstorm

The air is heavy with the passing storm.
The earth lies calm and free and glad again.
Through all its pores the flowering lilac bush
Drinks deep the pure cool freshness of the plain.

The world's reborn, transfigured by the storm.
The gutters shed a flood of rain. Now fair
And vast the blue beyond the shrouded sky,
And bright the ranges of celestial air.

But more exalted far the poet of power,
Who washes clean away the dust and grime,
When by his art emerge transformed the harsh
Realities and truths of naked time.

Then memories of lifetime sorrow fade
With passing storms. Free from their tutelage,
Our century proclaims it is high time
To clear a passage for the future age.

No swift upheaval swelling of itself
Will clear the way for our new age to be;
Our hope—the message of a spirit kindled
By truth, compassion, and magnanimity.

1958

Пронесшейся грозою полон воздух.
Всё ожило, всё дышит, как в раю.
Всем роспуском кистей лиловогроздых
Сирень вбирает свежести струю.

Всё живо переменою погоды.
Дождь заливает кровель жёлоба,
Но всё светлее неба переходы,
И высь за чёрной тучей голуба.

Рука художника ещё всесильней
Со всех вещей смывает грязь и пыль.
Преображёнными из его красильни
Выходят жизнь, действительность и быль.

Воспоминание о полувеке
Пронесшейся грозой уходит вспять.
Столетье вышло из его опеки.
Пора дорогу будущему дать.

Не потрясенья и перевороты
Для новой жизни очищают путь,
А откровенья, бури и щедроты
Души воспламенённой чьей-нибудь.

Весна 1958 г.
Переделкино.

Б. Пастернак

Winter Holidays

No future alone will content;
No present or past will delight.
We need the Eternal among us
With our Christmas tree tonight.

Then mother will trim our tree
And dress it with a silver star;
Brothers and sisters will flock
For the holiday feast from afar.

No matter what lacy trimmings
And spangles we hang on the guest,
We fancy our Christmas tree
Looks naked, empty, half-dressed.

In a billowing tinsel skirt
And a wisp of ruffled hair,
Our festive tree preens gaily
And puts on a lady's air.

At twelve, we're stiller than stone.
The shuddering candle light
Lingers on everyone's lips,
Like a heart, aglow in the night.

*   *   *

We'll joy for long until dawn.
To the slamming of cupboard doors,
The house will shake like a shack,
Then shudder loud with our snores.

Another twilight comes after
And the end of another day.
Our guests who gather for dinner
Have slept their noontime away.

Like a drunkard, the setting sun
Through a window-pane overhead
Will reach, in a flash of pleasure,
For the brandy glasses and bread;

Then slump like a brute on its face,
All bloated, in embers aglow,
And in hues of raspberry cordial
Sink fainter and darker in snow.

1959

Unique Days

Throughout the time of many winters
I recall each solstice and its days—
Each day unique, unlike another,
Repeated new in countless ways.

Here gradually the days become
A trail of winter snow and hoar—
Each day unique, so singular
That time appears to be no more.

I can recount them one by one:
The winter's halfway near its close,
The roads grow sodden, gutters drip,
The sun lies basking in the snows.

As in a dream, the lovers cling
Together in a long embrace;
High in the trees, in warmth again,
The starlings' cages sweat apace.

The arrows of the chiming clock
Now slower, half in slumber move;
Now longer than an age this day,
And longer my embrace of love.

1959

The Nobel Prize

Lost, like a cornered beast, I'm lost.
Somewhere people live in light,
Joy, and freedom. As for me,
I am hounded, trapped outright.

In a forest by a pond
I am like a levelled tree.
There is no escape. No matter.
Let the hunt and hunters be!

What the vile offence I've dared?
Am I a bandit out of hand,
I who made the world weep tears
Over beauty in my land?

None the less, I still believe,
Though I feel my death is near,
That the soul of men's goodwill
Will defeat all hate and fear.

January 1959

God's Great World

The evening shadows, fine as hair,
Move dreamily between the trees.
I meet our woman carrier
With mail for me from overseas.

By forest trails of fox and cat,
By tracks of cat and red fox trail,
I hurry home—to have a chat
At leisure with my friends by mail.

From islands, lakes, or mountain view,
Strange lands and continents, again
I talk, discuss, debate, review
With women, adolescents, men.

These men, I honor and revere!
What seasoned arguments behind
Their words, what proof of a sincere
And clear intelligence of mind!

And women's letters, precious too!
I've also tumbled from the spheres.
I'm thus in service bound to you
Today, tomorrow, all the years.

You stamp collectors too should know,
For every fleeting word of grace
What better gift could one bestow
Were you in my unlucky place!

1959

Notes and Comments

Page 4. *About My Verses*. Daryál, the great gorge in the Caucasus through which the Terek River flows, is the scene of Lermontov's best poetry. Lermontov (1814-41) was one whom Pasternak has admired most from his early youth. From him he learned that poetry must be expressive, true to life experience, but also faithful to eternal values. In *My Sister Life* (1922) Pasternak found himself in his own truthful, unique forms of expression. Lermontov's Demon, although a symbol of defiance and rebellion, was not altogether a Byronic rebel, but had Russian birthmarks. His revolt was interfused with melancholy, awareness of the tragedy of existence, and yearnings for love, peace, and perfection in the universal order. "What millennium have we today" was not a query prompted too seriously in a spirit of complete indifference to social affairs. Pasternak soon realized that the poetic imagination cannot remain aloof and indifferent to the dimensions of time and historic life, that the poet cannot evade his own age by escape from dead time ("To M. T."), and that he cannot shut out or transcend history without a sense of betrayal and guilt. ("There Is No One in That House").

Page 17. *Definition of Poetry*. Pasternak does not speak dogmatically about poetry, but gives instead a series of separate images. One of the definitions (the cry of a world at birth) may seem like a willful translation of the original text which says "tears of the world on a shoulder" (*v lopátkakh*). However in many regions of Russia common people speak of unshelled peas or beans in their pods as being *v lopátkakh*. Correctly interpreted it means then that poetry is the expression of the birthpangs of the new in the world.

Page 28. *Moochkap*. The name is that of a remote village at a small railway station in Tambov Province of central Russia. The watchful, excited mind of the observer and the details of the physical environment are intertwined, so that the effects are both visual and emotional.

Page 30. *Summer 1917*. Spiritual and physical details are blended in this poem as in a landscape painting. The poet accepts the Revolution as an event inherent in nature and in the soul of the common people, and he states that all classes, including the landowning gentry, were touched by the magic of new ideas of social harmony and dreams of brotherhood. In another poem, "So Be It," the Revolution is represented as a rifleshot, an eruption of nature; yet the poet is confident that the new day is a source of vitality and hope. His confidence in the new man, despite his vulgarity and insolence, is asserted in "January 1919," wherein the poet accepts the new with patience and humor and wisdom, in the belief that peace comes from men as it does from nature. In "Sailing Away" and in "We Are Few" the adventure into the unknown future, beyond established usage and institutions, finds an almost epic treatment.

Page 33. *Let's Strew Our Words*. In stanza 8 Yagáilo refers to the pagan Lithuanian prince (1348-1434) who married the young Polish queen Yadwíga, became king of Poland in 1386 and the founder of a new dynasty. The marriage brought about the union of the two countries. Yagáilo, and with him the whole of pagan Lithuania, embraced the Catholic faith. (The subject of the poem is the true poet, whose work is creative, spiritual, rich in details.)

Page 44. *A Theme With Variations*. The seven poems under this general title were originally known as Poems About Pushkin, written in celebration of the poet with particular reference to his narrative poem, *The Gypsies*. By reason of his African heritage, linked with European culture and education in the classics (the Imperial Lycée), Pushkin combined in his character primitive passion and disciplined creative power—two separate worlds fused in the man of genius. Pushkin is thus represented as the founder of a spiritual empire: 'tomorrows lived upon his lips as others lived with yesterdays.'

The Racing Stars, page 50, has for its subject the composition of Pushkin's *The Prophet*. The imagery is original and consistent. The poem is begun at night, within four walls of a room, and completed at dawn. But the setting is of world-wide, cosmic dimensions. The listening Sahara represents the growing consciousness of the poet; the smile of the wilderness, the joy of creative energy as the night wears away; the snoring Arkhangelsk, the poet's indifference to everything about him; dawn, the symbol of final achievement. These elements on both literal and symbolical levels are fused into one poetic act resembling the creative forces of nature itself. Pushkin's poem, a translation of which follows, has a large place in Russian literature and social thought.

My soul athirst for holy grace,
I wandered lone on desert ways,
And lo, there rose before my face
The angel of the Lord of Days.
He touched my eyes with fingers light
And soft as sleep at eventide;
My eyes became with vision wide,
Alarmed as eagles in the night.
He laid his finger on my ears,
And I heard a tumult fill the sky,
The sweep of angel wings on high;
I heard the trembling of the spheres,
The sap within the vines and trees,
And reptiles moving under seas.
He leaned above my mouth awhile
And tore from me my tongue of lust
And all its vanity and guile,
And with his bloody hand he thrust
Between my lips unmurmuring
And cold the serpent's subtle sting.
And with his sword he clove my breast,
And plucked my heart of fear and care,
And in my bosom rived and bare
A coal of living flame he pressed.
I lay upon the waste as dead.
And God called unto me and said:
"Arise, O prophet! Hear and see!
Fulfill my will, go forth again!
In every land, by every sea,
Burn with my words the hearts of men!"

Variations 4, 5 and 6 (pp. 51, 52 and 53) embody the dramatic
elements of *The Gypsies*. The subject is simple. Aleko, fleeing
the thraldom of stifling urban civilization, joins the gypsy bands
in Bessarabia. Zemfira takes him for her lover, and they live
together in her father's tent. After some time she falls in love
with a young gypsy. Aleko kills them in a fit of jealousy. The
gypsies deny him the right over a woman's affections and freedom.
(Jealousy? Murder?—'It never pays.') The old father addresses
Aleko in the tribe's name: "Leave us, proud man! . . . You are
not born for a free life. For yourself alone do you desire freedom!"
Civilized but possessive man, face to face with nature's humble

folk, is rejected as unworthy. Sea and stormwinds are here symbolic of the passions and splendor of gypsy life (p. 52: Ochakov is a Black Sea port, while Shabu and Kagul are settlements on the steppes). The camp moves on neath 'unspotted skies' and under eternal 'night of stars' (p. 53) leaving Aleko alone in the desert steppe.

Page 63. *Thus Life Begins*. Few poets have dared to express in a brief lyric, on a high level of symbolism, the fate of human beings from childhood to maturity under modern industrialism where the humble are beset by fears and anxieties, exploited by self-assertive careerists and adventurers. True, creative energies (poetry) set them on their way, but it often means a defiance of eternal values, while we give lip service to the Son of Man. Shelley, too, raised this issue in his unfinished *The Triumph of Life*. In his dream he watched the passage of great leaders and world conquerors—"hoary anarchs, demagogues, and sage"—and heard Rousseau say that "their power was given but to destroy."

Page 66. *In the Wood*. Poets often set love against the dread of fleeting time. But Pasternak holds that the two categories of experience and time are not divided in the organic structure of life. In this poem, the two lovers, on a physical plane, are in a state of satiety bordering on sleep. They are insensible to time, yet time persists in fact. Therefore, the poet constructs time symbolically. While the lovers sleep dreamlessly, the forces of nature construct a clock of their own, within the ether. In this manner we have the total fusion of nature, the lovers, and the infinite beyond in a single unity. The poem is both metaphysical and sensuous. Nature and poetry are thus welded together by subjecting nature to the discipline of poetry.

Page 69. *It's Spring Out There*. The poem may be taken as an epitome of Pasternak's method and thought. He builds, like a musician, a counterpoint of different sensuous themes—visual, auditory and emotional—such as poplar, house, air, a story begun by a star, and his own feelings about people. The central theme is that we live today in an ailing culture, in crumbling houses; that the story first begun by a star and once heard by man is now broken off; that we are in confusion, empty of mind and thought. These themes are not treated in absolute isolation, but they are joined together by a romantic note about the poplar tree that stands "amazed" at the sight of unnatural, alienated man.

Page 76. *Bloody Sunday.* This event marked the start of the Revolution of 1905. The government made use of security police and secret agents, especially the priest Gapon, popular among workers as a missionary and an eloquent speaker. To discourage independent political activity, he secretly organized groups of workers with monarchist leanings. At his suggestion, the striking workers organized a mass procession to the Winter Palace to lay a petition for redress before the Tsar. The workers were crushed by Cossack and infantry units with sabres and gunfire, leaving more than 1,000 dead and over 2,000 wounded. That event opened the way to terroristic acts. The Tsar's uncle, Grand Duke Sergéi Aleksándrovich Romanov (mentioned in the poem), governor general of Moscow and patron of the secondary school attended by young Pasternak, was killed by a bomb thrown by the socialist revolutionary I. Kalyáev.

Page 80. *Mutiny at Sea.* The Revolution of 1905 spread rapidly among the sailors of the Black Sea fleet. The revolt began on the battleship "Potémkin," where on June 27 the sailors were served stale food and wormy meat. The leaders were condemned to suffer severe discipline, but the crews liberated them, shot several officers, raised the Red flag, and placed themselves under the command of sailor Afanási Matushénko. The new commander directed the battleship to Odessa, where workers were engaged in street fights with police and troops.

Page 87. *A Testament.* Lieutenant Piótr Petróvich Schmidt (1867-1906) was the central figure at the sailors' uprising at Sebastopol in 1905. He was popular because of his democratic convictions and earnest dedication to liberal causes. The crews, including some infantry units, supported the workers at the naval base and in the city itself in the struggle with the military. On November 27 Lieutenant Schmidt went aboard the cruiser "Ochákov," intending to place himself at the head of the entire fleet, but only a few units raised the Red flag. The shore batteries remained loyal and fired on the rebel ships. Together with three other sailors, Schmidt was condemned to death by a military tribunal and shot on March 19 on the island of Berezan. The personality of the officer and the sea mutiny of the fleet inspired several writers and poets.

Lieutenant Schmidt's address before the military tribunal contained originally 11 stanzas and it was thus published in the May issue of *Novy Mir*, 1927. It is claimed in some quarters that the redaction to 7 stanzas was arbitrary and political in character. The earlier text is therefore given here in full:

In vain in days of chaos
We look for a happy end;
Some bear their Golgotha;
Some judge, and some repent.

Like you, I am an atom
In a time of transformation,
And I accept your verdict—
Resigned, without vexation.

I'm sure you will not falter
To sweep me off your stage,
O martyrs of your dogma,
O victims of your age!

For thirty years I've cherished
My country's destiny,
Yet I do not ask or hope for
Your magnanimity.

How vast the strife between
The things we know by name!
How dread the life we live
And suffer to our shame!

When men made out the end
Of bondage and abuse,

They learned your grant of rights
And justice was a ruse.

The people lose. The cause
You're ready to defend
Brings on, against your will,
Rebellion in the end.

The days we brood upon,
Remembering their roar,
Were days of surging waves
That hurled me to the fore.

It was hard to stand aloof,
And harder not to give
My life. I don't regret
The way I chose to live.

Though I stand above a chasm
By forces blind and drear,
I shall not cringe or yield;
My spirit shall not fear.

I stand between two eras
At war, and I rejoice:
The post between two camps
I occupy by choice.

Page 89. *Sublime Malady*. Pasternak once said that the poet must not distrust the living voice of life and truth, that art is like a sponge applied to the pattern of the race, that it continues the image of the race. This poem is a concentrated dramatic sketch of the epic that was the Revolution of 1917. It particularly reveals the failure of the conservative, liberal, and intellectual elements in a time of crisis. Pasternak condemns his own class of liberal thinkers who had no feeling for the image the masses had of themselves. He proudly embraces the positive leadership of men who acted as master builders, who opened the windows upon the future. The poem concludes with an evocation of Lenin as thinker and leader; he is referred to as *he* reverently—a man so great that he does not need a name. . . . The passage about 'two suns' in collision (page 97) relates to the end of tsarist Russia and the rise of revolutionary Soviet Union.'Dno' (here translated as Hollow Town) is the name of a small town in Pskov province; the abdication of Tsar Nicholas II took place in a railway train at that station, and the monarchy ended in a hollow, so to speak. 'Tosna' is a workingmen's settlement beside a small stream of that name, a few miles from Leningrad. The sun rising over Tosna stands for the rise of the new order of life.

Page 105. *The Soul.* The description of the soul as a true Tarak-ánova has reference to a historic personage, princess Tarakànova, who challenged the legal right of Catherine the Great to the throne. She died a prisoner in a fortress when her cell was flooded by the rising waters of the Neva.

Page 112. *To a Friend.* Pasternak sees the poet as a real force in national deliberative assemblies, as the people's spokesman, as a challenger to whom art and the practical life are undivided. In poetry and prose, Pasternak asserts the right of spiritual man to be "the voice of truth" without false idealization. He likes to quote Shakespeare's line about "art made tongue-tied by authority" (Sonnet LXVI). The state, demanding man's complete allegiance, must be faced by the poet who has an understanding of the totality of human values and experience. In fact, the state is in a sense faced with the poet in every man, because every man possesses his own uniqueness as a personality.

Page 113. *To Anna Akhmátova.* This name is the pseudonym of Anna Andréyevna Gorénko (b. 1888). Her love lyrics, published in 1912-15, established her universal reputation. Together with the poet Nikolai Gumilev, she became the leader of the Acmeist school of poetry, a movement founded in opposition to symbolist vagueness and mysticism. With the publication of her *Anno Domini* (1922), she practically closed her literary career, except for her studies of Pushkin, selections from her poetry books published in 1940, and a few patriotic poems in 1950. In the literary purge of 1946 Akhmátova's work was condemned, labeled as decadent and harmful to Soviet youth. The reference to the "pillar of salt" (stanza 7) is to Akhmátova's poem, "Lot's Wife"—the woman who paid with her life for taking one glance back, in her compassion for perishing humanity, upon the city which was her home. . . . New edition of her selected poetry, 1909-1960, appeared in 1961.

Page. 115. *To M. T.* The poem is dedicated to Marina Ivánovna

Tsvetáyeva (1892-1941), a major poet of the 'twenties. Her style was extraordinary, dynamic, staccato in its rhythms. An opponent of Bolshevism, she emigrated in 1922, but returned to the Soviet Union at the outbreak of the war in 1939, reconciled on patriotic grounds. She was evacuated from Moscow to the region of Kazan; there, in extreme poverty and ill health, she ended her life by hanging.

Page 124. *Lyubka*. This is a popular name for an uncommonly fragrant night violet, a small greenish-white flower found in woods and swampy places. Actually, it is of the orchid species, *orchis moris*, known among the common people as *dremlik* ("the dreamy one").

Page 132. *Socialism*. Pasternak was drawn to socialism by its creative forces, as a higher good. To socialism and the distant future he dedicated many poems (under general title *Waves*, 1932). He was fascinated by the Revolution and felt himself as its passive victim. Yet the Revolution became to him a sublime reality. He felt it was his duty to bear witness to his times as a poet, not as a camp follower; he refused to surrender to political pressure, to turn his poetry into a vehicle of propaganda. (*Putivl* in stanza 3 is the name of an ancient town in the region of Sumy, south of Novgorod Seversky; it has reference to the passage in *Lay of Igor's Campaign* in which princess Yaroslávna laments like a cuckoo the fate of her husband Igor.)

Page 135. *The Death of a Poet*. Vladimir Mayakovsky committed suicide in the morning of April 14, 1930. Pasternak's poem in his memory was first published in *Novy Mir*, January, 1931. In revised form, it was reprinted in his *Stikhotvoréniya* (Poems), edition 1933. Later, in 1957, in preparing a new edition, the poet deleted four lines for purely esthetic reasons.

Page 151. *Hurry, My Verses, Hurry!* Gogol's *Viy*, page 152 refers to title of a story of romantic weirdness mingled with superstition and ruthless humor.

Page 156. *Ages. He Appears*. The term 'Ghelaty' in stanza 1 refers to the famous ancient monastery in Georgia, a religious cultural center in the Caucasus. The place is associated with King David the Builder.

Page 167. *A Sentimental Waltz*. "Waltz With Tears" is the literal title, but it means a melody (waltz), a sentimental celebration. The details are material and concrete, suggesting affluence and the holiday spirit, but at same time an eternal tradition.

Page 179. *The Poems of Dr. Zhivago.* This group of 25 poems, the appendix of the novel, is the key to Zhivago's vision of life and Pasternak's own attitude towards love, revolution, society, life. Their order is organic and harmonic, not strictly chronological.

(1) *Hamlet* belongs to a series dealing with urban life. Pasternak understands Hamlet as a drama of duty and self-sacrifice, called upon to 'do the will of the one that sent him.' Through his dead father Hamlet had an intimate personal relationship with the Eternal. It was a challenge which he accepted voluntarily as an expression of man's spiritual freedom; he accepted the bitter cup, as must the poet, the man with a mission and a special responsibility from times immemorial, as a means of addressing himself to humanity.

(2) Spring is personified by a bustling milkmaid, her hands loaded with work (*March*). In the same cycle *Holy Week* is a revelation of the miracle of the ressurrection and the teachings of Christ by which 'death shall be destroyed' through love and suffering. History, in Zhivago's opinion, is a living chain of love joining all generations of men, and Christ is its first link. *White Night* is the first love poem, the fate of the lovers being bound up with the destiny of the city, its past and future. *Spring Thaw*, an expression of ecstacy, grief, and fate, belongs to the time in Zhivago's life when he moved to the Urals.

(3) The summer cycle is brief. The poems are highly personal, concerned with the transcendental meaning of everyday life. It includes *Summer in the City* and *Intoxication*, both sensuous in mood. (Hops and intoxication are known, in Russian, by the noun *khmel*). The poem *False Summer* is familial in tone; it celebrates the joys of domestic activities in the country. The cycle concludes with the joyous *Wedding Party*, a rhapsodic affirmation of work, marriage and love, wherein divided selves joined as one with other selves find their blessing as a precious gift, as a song,—a dove winging in the blue.

(4) The glow of the poem *Autumn* provides a background for a life of intense passion, doomed from the start, and fateful estrangement from the world. It is followed by the *Fairy Tale*, in which the knight and the maiden struggle against tyranny. It is the poetic record of Zhivago's life, a symbolic narrative of the

individual struggle against force and chance in the world, and of the inevitable silent triumph of love.

(5) In the winter cycle, the personality of Lara rules the life of Zhivago either directly or symbolically in the poems *Winter Night, Parting, Meeting,* and *Mary Magdalene.*

(6) After the tragedies of despair and loss, the renewal of hope is introduced by the purely Christian cycle dealing with the love of God for man and man's love of God and all created things: *Star of the Nativity, Dawn, Earth, August, The Miracle, Evil Days,* and *Garden of Gethsemane.* (In *August,* the phrase 'days of dull despair' in stanza 11 stands for the untranslatable noun *bezvremén-shchina,* meaning a state of apathy, spiritual letdown, a life without the sense of the timeless; it is a despair which comes from the sin of *acedia,* a sin against love, a kind of sad dejection of mind and spirit.) The identification of the individual with the masses, stay-at-homes, children and trees (*Dawn*) makes up the theme of Christian service in the cause of the nameless; by that sign alone man apprehends his 'sole true victory' in life and his true immortality. *Dawn* is addressed to a mysterious Thou; it is the godlike aspect present in the character and destiny of the Russian people as revealed by her foremost novelists and poets. We are reminded here of Christ who came to bring the Kingdom of God into the world, and who died on the cross. By taking his place behind Doctor Zhivago, Pasternak affirms man's conquest of death through love and faith, the triumph of life over dogma and social hatreds in the struggle against the Pharisees of the totalitarian age.

Page 231. *When the Skies Clear.* This cycle of 44 poems (*Kogdá razguliáyetsa*) represent Pasternak's last poetry, 1956 to January 1959. Feeling at home, secure in his own artistic conscience, Pasternak now stands closest to the main traditions of Russian realism by addressing himself to his readers with the quiet passion and detachment characteristic of Pushkin. With such contemporaries as Blok and Mayakovsky, Pasternak thus becomes the true inheritor of the great traditions of Russian lyricism and philosophy of art.

EUGENE M. KAYDEN